BIGFOOT HUNTERS GUIDE

A Field Manual for Modern Sasquatch Investigation

By

Timothy D

Copyright © 2023 by Timothy D

All rights reserved.

No portion of this book may be reproduced in any form without written permission from the publisher or author, except as permitted by U.S. and Canadian copyright laws.

This publication is designed to provide accurate and authoritative information in regard to the subject matter covered. While the publisher and author have used their best efforts in preparing this book, they make no representations or warranties with respect to the accuracy or completeness of the contents of this book. The advice and strategies contained herein may not be suitable for your situation. You should consult with a professional when appropriate. Neither the publisher nor the author shall be liable for any loss including but not limited to special, incidental, consequential, personal, or other damages.

Book Cover by Timothy D

Illustrations by Timothy D

2nd revised edition 2025

Table of Contents

Introduction: Embarking on Your Bigfoot Research Journey

1. The Bigfoot Phenomenon: Folklore, Sightings, and Legends
2. What could Bigfoot be?
3. Common misconceptions about Bigfoot
4. Bigfoot are known by a variety of names
5. Famous Bigfoot Sightings and Encounters
6. Well Known Vocalizations:
7. How Natives describe Bigfoot
8. Bigfoot Hotspots and Habitats around the world
9. North America Hotspots:
10. Bigfoot Hotspots in Asia
11. Here are some steps you can take to get started if you're interested in becoming a Bigfoot researcher
12. Bigfoot Research Techniques and Strategies
13. The Researcher's Field Gear
14. Tracking and Field Techniques
15. Track Casting in Bigfoot Research
16. Field Audio recording
17. Safety of Bigfoot Researchers
18. What information should be recorded in field notes
19. Witness Interview Procedures in Bigfoot Research
20. What attracts a Bigfoot?
21. What time of day are you most likely to encounter a bigfoot or bigfoot vocalization?
22. Analyzing Evidence and Differentiating Bigfoot Signs
23. Best Practices for Setting Up Basecamp in the Wilderness
24. Using GoPro cameras or similar.
25. How to Optimize Placement of Trail Cameras
26. Collaboration and Community in Bigfoot Research
27. Speaking to Authorities about Bigfoot Knowledge
28. Theory on the Migration of Bigfoot
29. Using Drones for Bigfoot Research
30. Collecting DNA samples in the field
31. Using Social Media
32. Using YouTube
33. Google Maps and Google Earth
34. Bigfoot hoaxers and pranksters
35. Top Ten Scientists Conducting Bigfoot Research
36. Top Ten Bigfoot Researchers
37. Top Bigfoot Research Groups
38. Famous Quotes and Reflections on Bigfoot
39. State and Provincial Bigfoot Hotspots

Introduction: Embarking on Your Bigfoot Research Journey

Welcome to the world of Bigfoot research, where the shadows of ancient forests and the mysteries of the unknown converge. This guide is your compass, your field guide,  and your source of knowledge as you set foot on a path that has captivated seekers of the extraordinary for generations. For those who have just begun their quest and for those who have long been entranced by the allure of the enigmatic, this guide aims to condense years of research into your hands, providing you with a comprehensive starting point that will save you precious time and effort.

In your pursuit of the elusive creature known as Bigfoot, this guide is designed to equip you with the fundamental tools, methodologies, and insights required to navigate a realm that straddles the borders of science, folklore, and wonder. It serves as both a primer and a reference, catering to your curiosity while steering you away from the pitfalls and dead ends that have consumed the efforts of many before you.

As you delve into the chapters ahead, you will discover a curated compilation of essential knowledge that spans the history, cultural significance, field techniques, and evolving science surrounding Bigfoot. Whether you're exploring the depths of the forest with camera in hand, sifting through footprint evidence, or engaging in spirited debates with fellow researchers, this guide aims to empower you with a foundational understanding that ignites your passion and guides your exploration.

Remember, embarking on this journey requires an open mind, a critical eye, and a willingness to embrace the unknown. While definitive answers about Bigfoot's existence remain elusive, the pursuit of knowledge and the quest for truth are endeavours that enrich our understanding of the world and our place within it.

So, let this guide be your companion as you embark on your Bigfoot research journey —a journey that might just lead you to uncover secrets hidden within the depths of the wilderness and, perhaps, save you years of research while laying the groundwork for your own contributions to this fascinating field of exploration.

Chapter 1

The Bigfoot Phenomenon: Folklore, Sightings, and Legends

As we explore the realm of Bigfoot hunting in more detail, it's critical to comprehend the complex web of stories, sightings, and mythology that has given rise to this persistent phenomena. This chapter peels back the layers of the Bigfoot story to show the stories that have stoked our collective imagination, from old tales to modern experiences.

Folklore Across Cultures

Bigfoot, who goes by several names in different cultures, has had a lasting impression on indigenous peoples' and communities' mythologies all across the world. These enigmatic characters—from the Yowie of Australia to the Yeti of the Himalayas—have a mystery, wilderness, and inexplicable quality in common. Examining these cultural differences reveals more about the persistent human curiosity with concealed beings.

Sightings: From Anecdotes to Anomalies

The large number of sightings that people from all walks of life have recorded form the foundation of the Bigfoot phenomena. Although the veracity of eyewitness reports varies, they all relate to the same event: a brief sighting of a massive, humanoid monster in the woods. Each sighting adds another level of complexity to the Bigfoot enigma, ranging from clear views to in-depth descriptions.

Modern Legends and Pop Culture

Contemporary media and popular culture have had a profound impact on the emergence of the Bigfoot phenomena. From shaky video footage to dramatic documentaries, Bigfoot's transformation from a secretive woodland creature to a cultural icon has been documented. Analyzing the ways in which media representations have both supported and refuted the legend provides an intriguing window into the intersection of folklore and contemporary culture.

Examining the Evidence: Footprints, Audio, and Visuals

As seekers of truth, Bigfoot hunters meticulously analyze the evidence left behind by the elusive creature. This section delves into the scientific scrutiny applied to various forms of evidence, shedding light on the complexities and challenges of evaluating Bigfoot's presence in the natural world.

Footprints: Imprints of a Mystery

Bigfoot footprints, one of the most recognizable pieces of evidence, have been found in a variety of settings. Specialists examine these prints closely to look for anatomical features, walking habits, and other traits that could identify the animal. Even with recent technological developments, it is still difficult to tell real prints from fakes.

Audio Recordings: Voices in the Wilderness

Researchers are interested in Bigfoot because of his eerie sounds and vocalizations. Experts try to determine whether sounds are caused by recognized animals, human influence, or something else different by listening to recordings. Even while the audio evidence is powerful, it presents difficulties for validation and interpretation.

Visuals: Through the Lens of Cameras

Images and recordings purporting to show Bigfoot sightings have divided and inspired the study community. These images, which range from the renowned Patterson-Gimlin film to contemporary smartphone footage, have two opposing effects: they both hint at a possible monster while also raising questions and demanding closer examination.

Chapter 2

What could Bigfoot be?

Unknown Primate Species: Many Bigfoot researchers speculate that Bigfoot could be an undiscovered or unrecognized species of primate. They often point to the creature's reported ape-like characteristics, such as its bipedal walking and large size.

Gigantopithecus: Some researchers suggest that Bigfoot could be a surviving population of Gigantopithecus Blacki, an extinct ape species that lived in Asia. While Gigantopithecus was indeed a large primate, there is limited fossil evidence, and it's unclear if it could have lived in the environments reported for Bigfoot sightings.

Hominin Species: Another theory is that Bigfoot could be a type of hominid, a branch of the evolutionary tree that includes humans and our closest relatives. Proponents of this idea suggest that Bigfoot might be a relic population of a previously unknown hominin species.

Hoaxes and Misidentifications: Skeptics and mainstream scientists often point out that many Bigfoot sightings can be attributed to misidentifications of known animals, such as bears, or even hoaxes perpetrated by individuals seeking attention or profit.

Inter-dimensional or Paranormal Theories: Some Bigfoot researchers propose more speculative ideas, suggesting that Bigfoot might have inter-dimensional or paranormal abilities that allow it to evade detection or appear and disappear at will. These theories tend to be more fringe and lack scientific support.

Ancient Human Relatives: Another hypothesis is that Bigfoot could be a relict population of an ancient human relative that survived long after their presumed extinction. This idea is often not supported by mainstream anthropological evidence.

Chapter 3

Common misconceptions about Bigfoot:

1. **Physical Evidence Is Definitive**: Despite the fact that some physical evidence, such as footprints and hair samples, have been linked to Bigfoot, they are frequently erroneous, the result of fabrication, or are affected by other circumstances. Using only physical evidence without considering context or proper interpretation can be misleading.

2. **There Is Only One Species of Bigfoot**: Many other enormous, bipedal cryptid monsters are referred to as "Bigfoot" in this way. There may not be a single "Bigfoot" species, though, as other cultures and geographical areas have their own myths and names for such creatures.

3. **Bigfoot Always Leaves Visible Evidence**: It's a common myth that Bigfoot always leaves visible evidence, such as distinct footprints. In fact, many stories are based on short glances, far-off sightings, or vague indications.

4. **Bigfoot Is Always hostile or Dangerous**: Despite some accounts of Bigfoot being hostile or dangerous, no recurring pattern of violent behaviour has been linked to them. The majority of accounts speak of elusive, shy creatures who avoid interacting with people.

5. **Bigfoot Would Be Easily Discovered**: Some people think that if Bigfoot existed, it would have been positively identified by now because of developments in technology and the popularity of outdoor enthusiasts. The creature's secretive nature, alleged intellect, and the size of wilderness areas, though, could all help it stay undetected.

6. **All Reports of Bigfoot Sightings Are Valid**: The sheer volume of sightings reported does not necessarily imply the veracity of the encounters. The amount of sightings can be exacerbated by misidentifications, exaggerations, and even intentional hoaxes, making it difficult to assess the veracity of each sighting.

7. **Everyone Accepts the Existence of Bigfoot**: Despite the great interest in Bigfoot, mainstream society, academics, and scientists do not concur that the creature exists.

Skepticism has spread widely due to a lack of convincing evidence and the impact of pranks.

8. **Bigfoot Fits Neatly into Scientific Categories**: If Bigfoot exists, some people believe that it would fit into established scientific categories. The existence of such a species, however, might call into question long-held beliefs about biology, evolution, and primate behaviour.

9. **All Bigfoot Researchers Are the Same**: There are many different types of bigfoot researchers, from serious scientists to ardent amateurs. It is crucial to distinguish between serious researchers and sensationalists because the area comprises a diverse variety of methodology, viewpoints, and strategies.

10. **Bigfoot Is Just a Myth or Legend**: While skepticism is healthy, ignoring the intricacy of the phenomena and labelling all Bigfoot claims as just myths or legends is not. Even if they don't conclusively demonstrate the creature's existence, there are several cases of sightings and evidence that remain unexplained.

It's crucial to keep an open mind when discussing Bigfoot while also critically analyzing the available data and assertions. It takes serious thought, investigation, and the ability to accept doubt where it exists to tell fact from fiction.

Chapter 4

Bigfoot is given a variety of names in various countries and cultures. Here is a list of some of the names given to similar animals:

Sasquatch: The name used primarily in North America, especially in the Pacific Northwest. "Sasquatch" is derived from the Halkomelem language of indigenous peoples in that region.

Yeti: Also known as the "Abominable Snowman," the Yeti is a legendary ape-like creature said to inhabit the Himalayan mountains, primarily in Nepal and Tibet.

Yowie: This name is used in Australia to describe a creature similar to Bigfoot. Yowie legends are prominent in Aboriginal Australian mythology.

Almas: A name used in Central Asia, particularly in Mongolia and Kazakhstan. The Almas is described as a wild man or ape-like creature.

Mande Barung: This name is associated with a cryptid from the remote northeastern Indian state of Assam. The Mande Barung is said to be a large ape-like creature.

Skunk Ape: A term used in the southeastern United States, particularly in Florida. The Skunk Ape is said to emit a strong odor, similar to a skunk.

Orang Pendek: A creature said to inhabit the dense forests of Sumatra, Indonesia. "Orang Pendek" means "short person" in Indonesian, and descriptions often resemble a small, upright ape.

Mapinguari: A legendary creature from South American folklore, particularly in the Amazon rainforest. The Mapinguari is often depicted as a giant sloth-like creature.

Sabie: is a legendary, ape-like cryptid said to inhabit the forests of South Africa, often described as large, hairy, and elusive.

Chuchunya: From Russian folklore, the Chuchunya is described as a large, hairy hominid. Sightings have been reported in the remote Siberian wilderness.

Barmanou: Said to inhabit the mountains of Pakistan and Afghanistan, the Barmanou is often described as a large, hairy creature with human-like features.

Nguoi Rung: The "Forest People" of Vietnam, Nguoi Rung is a term used to describe creatures resembling Bigfoot that are said to inhabit the country's forests.

Yeren: In addition to the Chinese Yeren, this term is also used in Vietnam to describe a wild, human-like creature rumored to live in the forests.

Wendigo: While not exactly a Bigfoot-like creature, the Wendigo is a mythical creature from Algonquian folklore in North America. It is often associated with cannibalism and winter.

Maricoxi: A creature from South American indigenous lore, particularly among the Yanomami people of the Amazon rainforest. The Maricoxi is often described as a large, hairy, and aggressive being.

Nuk-luk: In the Inuit mythology of northern Canada, the Nuk-luk is a fearsome, hairy creature said to inhabit the wilderness.

Agogwe: From the legends of the African Pygmies, the Agogwe is believed to be a small, human-like creature with long hair.

Momo: Short for "Missouri Monster," Momo is the name given to a Bigfoot-like creature that was reported to inhabit Missouri, USA, in the 1970s.

Nandi Bear: A cryptid reported in East Africa, particularly among the Nandi people of Kenya. Descriptions vary, but it's often described as a large, aggressive bear-like creature.

Orang Dalam: A cryptid from Malaysian and Indonesian folklore, the Orang Dalam is described as a humanoid creature living in the forests.

Kaptar: In Turkic mythology, the Kaptar is a wild, hairy creature similar to Bigfoot, often associated with mountainous regions.

Mogollon Monster: Reported in Arizona and New Mexico, USA, the Mogollon Monster is said to resemble Bigfoot and is named after the Mogollon Rim.

Chaneques: In Mexican folklore, the Chaneques are small, mischievous creatures that are sometimes described as having hairy or ape-like features.

Enkidu: From ancient Mesopotamian mythology, Enkidu is a wild man created by the gods to challenge the protagonist Gilgamesh in the epic of Gilgamesh.

Tornit: In Inuit mythology, the Tornit is a race of powerful, hairy giants that live in the mountains and are known for their strength.

Batutut: A creature reported in the Philippines, the Batutut is described as a small, hairy humanoid with long hair covering its entire body.

Sisemite: From Native American Yokut mythology in California, the Sisemite is a giant, ape-like creature that inhabits the mountains.

Chapter 5

Famous Bigfoot Sightings and Encounters

We'll look at some of the most well-known Bigfoot sightings in this chapter, along with encounter tales that have added to the ongoing obsession with this mythical creature. These tales have provoked discussion and interest, which has encouraged scientists and enthusiasts to look for proof of Bigfoot's existence.

The Patterson-Gimlin Film (1967)

The Enigmatic Encounter - The Long-Lasting Influence of the Patterson-Gimlin Film Few individuals are as well-known in the history of cryptozoology as Roger Patterson and Bob Gimlin, two daring explorers whose lives were eternally linked to the mysterious Bigfoot legend. The untamed expanses of Bluff Creek, California, hid secrets that would captivate the world in 1967, a moment of adventure and inquiry. During this time, the two set out on a quest that would make history and turn a mysterious creature by the name of "Patty" into a recognizable figure in the world of Bigfoot sightings.

The Expedition: A Quest for the Unknown

Roger Patterson and Bob Gimlin were not experienced researchers or scientists. They were ordinary people drawn together by a passion for the legends of a gigantic, hairy bipedal creature that prowled the forests of the Pacific Northwest. They set off for Bluff Creek, a beautiful but enigmatic wilderness that had become a hotspot for suspected Bigfoot activity, with a camera in hand and a drive to uncover the truth behind the legend.

The pair's expedition was motivated by a combination of anxiety and anticipation. They trudged through thick underbrush and over rocky routes with their 16mm camera and a steadfast desire to capture the unusual, led by the whispers of the unknown. As they travelled further into the uninhabited wilderness, days turned into nights and the distinction between fact and fiction started to get hazy.

Encounter at Bluff Creek: The Birth of a Legend

On a brisk autumn morning, destiny brought Patterson and Gimlin together, permanently cementing their place in the history of cryptozoology. Their camera lens caught an event that would spark discussions, enquires, and skepticism for decades to come in a clearing among the tall trees. The shape of the beast spoken about around campfires was startlingly similar to the large, shaggy figure that strode briskly across the clearing.

The footage, which is now infamously known as the Patterson-Gimlin film, featured a creature that was given the name "Patty" by individuals who carefully examined the footage. Patty, a tall, strong bipedal creature with dark hair and an uncanny grace, moved inexplicably gracefully. Her quick glance toward the camera seemed to be bearing the weight of ages, hinting at the enigma she represented.

The Controversy and the Turning Point

The Patterson-Gimlin movie propelled Bigfoot into the public eye while also igniting a heated discussion that alienated both believers and skeptics. Due to issues with the creature's size and the limitations of 1960s technology, some questioned the film's validity. The video, according to its critics, was just a scam created with expensive costumes and special effects.

In the face of the onslaught of doubt, Patterson and Gimlin held firm, resolute in their claim that what they had recorded was an actual meeting. Although heated, the discussion brought Bigfoot research to the fore and reignited interest in the study of cryptids and the natural world's mysteries.

Legacy and Ongoing Inquiry

The Patterson-Gimlin movie is still a recognizable landmark in the field of cryptozoology decades after that fatal encounter. Patty, captured in a few fleeting seconds of film, has come to represent the search for the uncharted, the allure of the wild, and the undeniable allure of uncovering the mysteries that still lurk within the uncharted regions of our globe.

The Patterson-Gimlin movie marks a turning moment in the investigation of Bigfoot, whether it be due to real evidence or skillful deception. It keeps creating conversations that fan the flames of discovery and inspiring both professional scientists and curious minds. The voyage of Patterson and Gimlin serves as a reminder that the search for the enigmatic transcends the commonplace and that, occasionally, the most profound truths can be discovered deep within the wilderness.

Famous Bigfoot Sightings and Encounters cont'd

The Ape Canyon Incident (1924)

It was 1924, a period when the soaring woods of the Pacific Northwest held enigmatic truths that had been whispered throughout history. A gang of miners set out on a journey that would permanently inscribe their names into the annals of cryptid lore deep within the untamed wilderness near Mount St. Helens in Washington State. This is the account of the astonishing and terrifying Ape Canyon experience, which helped to establish Bigfoot as a legendary creature of the wild.

A Group of Prospectors and the Isolation of Ape Canyon

Five miners made a life out of the wilderness high in the Cascade Mountains. The unexpected group of individuals—Fred Beck, Gabe Lefever, John Peterson, Marion Smith, and Smith's son Roy—would soon find themselves at the centre of an astonishing story. In a distant and ominous place now known as Ape Canyon, these prospectors had staked their claims and constructed their improvised cabin. Ape Canyon got its name from the strange echoes that seemed to reverberate through its cavernous depths.

The Encounters Begin: Mysterious Creatures and Hurling Rocks

It began as eerie murmurs in the darkness, dancing at the edges of their perceptions. The miners' dogs felt it as well; their hackles stood up as though tuned in to something lurking just beyond the glow of their campfire. The rumours eventually became a terrifying reality as time went on.

The miners' haven was surrounded by a cacophony of disorder one fateful night. Huge pebbles came flying through the air, hitting with a ferocity that defied description against the walls of their shelter. The miners huddled in dread, trying to make sense of the origin of this bizarre attack. The aftermath, which included enormous footprints that were imprinted around their hut like a mark left behind, made it clear how tremendous the attack had been when dawn broke and the dust settled.

Confrontation with the Unknown: The Battle of Ape Canyon

The miners' initial fear quickly gave way to resolve as they swore to protect their land from the mysterious aliens that appeared to be trying to drive them out. They got ready for a fight that would test their mettle and blur the lines between reality and the unknown, armed with guns and steely nerves.
The miners would later describe these animals as being huge, hairy, and like apes as they engaged in a series of terrifying encounters over the course of several nights. The clashes were tense as the miners fired their rifles into the night, their bullets appearing to be deflected by the tenacity of their attackers. They were both disturbed and inspired by each encounter, a tribute to humanity's persistent spirit in the face of the inexplicable

Legacy and Impact: Strengthening the Bigfoot Mythos

The Ape Canyon incident marked a turning point in the development of Bigfoot mythology. The miners' accounts, which were supported by their vivid depictions of large, hostile monsters and the uncannily well-coordinated rock-throwing assaults, shocked the Pacific Northwest and beyond. As the lines between myth and truth again blurred, the story sparked curiosity, speculating, and plenty of doubt.
The strange energies that flow through the woods are still evident today in Ape Canyon, inspiring both awe and dread. The miners' tale serves as a reminder that there are still unexplored areas and mysteries that defy simple explanation, even in the current era. The Ape Canyon incident is more than just a chapter in the Bigfoot tale; it offers a window into the primordial core of the unfathomable, a setting where people and the wild coexist in a dance that is beyond comprehension.

Famous Bigfoot Sightings and Encounters cont'd

The Albert Ostman Encounter (1924)

A Captive Among Giants

In 1924, a story took place in the deep woods of British Columbia that would forever leave a mark on the fabric of Bigfoot lore. This is the unusual tale of prospector Albert Ostman, whose routine search for wealth turned into a stunning meeting with mysterious creatures who inhabit the periphery of human comprehension.

Quest for Riches and Unforeseen Abduction

Albert Ostman, a man of unwavering resolve and steadfast spirit, set his sights on the unexplored regions of British Columbia in search of priceless minerals buried beneath the surface of the planet. He set out into the bush with his prospecting equipment and a desire for adventure, not realizing that his journey would soon take him into the mysterious.

Ostman found himself in a scenario he could never have imagined as the days changed into nights and the wilderness loomed all around him. One night, he was startled from his sleep by a strange presence—a horde of towering beings that defied all description. He was swept away by these aliens before he could understand the situation, not by their force but more by their sheer physical superiority.

The Family of Giants: A Bizarre Bond

The experience of being held captive by the creatures that Ostman would later refer to as Bigfoot was bizarre and contradicted his perception of reality. He was being confined in a location that seemed to exist outside of time, among a family of creatures that inspired both fear and amazement. These creatures were unlike anything he had ever seen before; they were gigantic in stature, covered in hair, and possessed a primitive intelligence that communicated with a universe beyond the realm of human cognition.

Weeks passed by as Ostman's encounters with the Bigfoot family evolved into a peculiar mingling of captivity and shared interest. He watched their motions, how they interacted with one another, and how they maneuvered around their environment in a simple yet sophisticated way. Ostman's opinion on these beings started to change as his initial anxiety gave way to an odd friendship, exposing layers of complexity that defied preconceptions.

Escape and Legacy: Unraveling the Enigma

Ostman's escape from the Bigfoot family's grasp was equally bizarre as his first kidnapping. He was able to escape his captors and return to the world of humans by seizing the chance to do so. When his narrative was revealed, it elicited responses ranging from fascination to cynicism. Ostman's vivid descriptions of his encounters with Bigfoot creatures sparked discussions and arguments that went beyond the bounds of conventional comprehension.

Others were fascinated by the idea that mankind coexisted with creatures that defied simple classification, while some people disregarded his story as an elaborate fiction. Ostman's encounter strengthened the Bigfoot myth, adding depth to the creatures' existence and rekindling the interest of individuals who dared to contemplate the mysteries concealed in the Earth's wild places.

Famous Bigfoot Sightings and Encounters cont'd

The Ruby Creek Bigfoot Encounter

The Ruby Creek wilderness is located in the farthest corners of British Columbia, where the forests hold ancient tales and the rivers whisper secrets. A fable that would go down in the annals of Bigfoot lore was formed amid the soaring trees and secret valleys. This is the account of the Bigfoot sighting at Ruby Creek, when the line separating the real world from the paranormal seemed to dissolve in the presence of a mysterious giant.

The Isolated Beauty of Ruby Creek

Ruby Creek's unspoiled beauty belied the secrets that lingered beneath its serene exterior. Ruby Creek is located deep within the untamed embrace of the Canadian backwoods. The area's isolation and unspoiled wilderness drew explorers, adventurers, and people looking for a haven from the bustle of contemporary life. Yet something awaited behind the towering evergreens, a mysterious presence that captured the curiosity of both residents and tourists.

The Encounter: A Glimpse into the Unseen

A team of daring explorers headed out with the straightforward objective of taking in Ruby Creek's untamed magnificence in the middle of this wilderness. What started off as a voyage of reverence and amazement would quickly transform into an encounter that defied explanation.

The adventurers set up camp one fateful evening as the sun set behind the mountains and shadows danced across the terrain. They first noticed something that would permanently change their understanding of reality in the quiet minutes of dusk. A tall, cloaked in hair figure with a primeval aura that seemed to resound across the ages emerged from the forest's depths.

A Silent Exchange

A brief contact between the known and the unknown occurred as the explorers and the mysterious figure locked eyes. Bigfoot, as it was generally known, stood like a sentinel of mystery, inspiring both fascination and a deep, unspoken understanding. The mutual recognition that two distinct worlds—one formed by human experience and the other by the uncontrolled forces of nature—were merging was reflected in the fixed gazes.

The apparition then vanished into the shadows just as quickly as it had emerged, leaving the explorers in amazement and shock. They talked quietly as they shared their experiences because they believed that speaking aloud might break the thin barrier separating their world from the realm of the unknown.

The Ripple Effect

The Bigfoot sighting at Ruby Creek became a rumoured legend, a story passed down through the centuries like a sacred fire. As the story spread, other sightings and encounters were reported, creating a picture of a monster that defied simple classification. Although there were arguments between believers and skeptics, the crux of the mystery—the wild unknown—remains at the limits of human comprehension.

A reminder that even in the modern era of knowledge and technology, the wild regions still hold secrets that defy explanation, Ruby Creek's tale expanded through time. The Ruby Creek encounter became more than simply a one-off occurrence; it became evidence of the ongoing pull of the mysterious, the untamed, and the potential that ancient voices still reverberate in the shadows.

Famous Bigfoot Sightings and Encounters cont'd

The Sierra Sounds (1970s)

Echoes in the Wilderness - The Enigma of the Sierra Sounds

A mysterious song carried on the winds evolved into an unanticipated symphony of mystery nestled within the untamed expanses of the Sierra Nevada mountains. The Sierra Sounds, an enigmatic auditory phenomenon that resonated throughout the woods and sparked the imagination of those who ventured to listen, are the subject of this tale.

The Sierra Nevada's Secret World

Whispers of the unknown have long braided their way into local legend in the Sierra Nevada's high peaks and deep woods. Generations of people have been told stories about creatures that live in remote locations and provide a window into a world that transcends human comprehension. The Sierra Sounds originally appeared in this environment, capturing the attention of those who dared to investigate the wild heart of California.

Whispers in the Night: The Discovery of the Sounds

A mysterious and unpleasant occurrence was discovered by hunter and outdoor enthusiast Al Berry in the early 1970s. When Berry was camping out in the Sierra Nevada backcountry, a series of vocalizations that echoed throughout the night scared him. To his trained ears, they were not the noises of creatures he knew; they were guttural, spooky, and entirely foreign.

Berry, interested and unaffected, started out on a mission to record these mysterious noises. With audio equipment in hand, he frequently entered the forest and captured a symphony of screams that seemed to defy classification. The resulting collection of recordings—known as the Sierra Sounds—spurred speculation and speculations about their origin.

The Bigfoot Connection: A Sonorous Enigma

The vocalizations that are usually linked to Bigfoot sightings remarkably resemble the wild timbre and unsettling resonance of the Sierra Sounds. The sound recordings immersed listeners in a world where reality and fiction were blurred. The hypothesis that a hidden population of Bigfoot creatures was responsible for these noises gained popularity and provoked discussions among specialists, believers, and skeptics.

Al Berry's encounters with these mysterious animals were recorded on tape, and those conversations revealed patterns that mirrored the communication challenges. The Sierra Sounds seemed to indicate not just a kind of artistic expression but also a glimpse into the social organization of a mysterious world where enigmatic species engaged in behaviours that were hard for humans to fathom.

Legacy and Legacy: Echoes That Persist

Like the wild place they came from, the Sierra Sounds remained a mystery. Others learned that they were the echoes of a mysterious secret that had been proclaimed on the winds, reverberating from the depths of an ancient forest, while some attempted to explain them away as ingenious pranks or the screams of well-known monsters.

The mystery surrounding the Sierra Sounds resonates across the Bigfoot legend community as a terrifying reminder that there are still untamed and unknown regions even in our age of technological advancements. The Sierra Nevada's mesmerizing sounds pay aural homage to the wild's enduring appeal and people's unwavering drive to discover truths that lay beyond the boundaries of the known.

Famous Bigfoot Sightings and Encounters cont'd

The 2000 Green Swamp Encounter

In the year 2000, a story from the enormous and enigmatic Green Swamp of Florida came to light that would have an impact on the field of cryptozoology. This is the story of the Green Swamp Encounter, a terrifying eyewitness encounter that brought the idea of Bigfoot into the heart of the southeastern wilderness and out of the Pacific Northwest.

Uncharted Wilderness of the Green Swamp

The Green Swamp is a vast area of marshes, cypress groves, and dense vegetation that is tucked away in central Florida. Its complex network of canals and lush vegetation is home to a wide variety of wildlife, including the elusive and infrequently seen Florida panther. A mysterious beast that had been discussed in whispers for decades was rumoured to be roaming this area, though.

The Eerie Night in the Swamp

A group of friends set out on a journey that would forever alter their understanding of the natural world on a moonlight night in the year 2000. They made camp deep into the Green Swamp, surrounded by the eerie chorus of nocturnal creatures. They had no idea what was going to happen when they encountered the unknown.

Unease descended upon the group as the bonfire flickered and the air was filled with the many sounds of the marsh. The night appeared to be holding its breath as branches snapped and the underbrush rustled. Then, as if emerging from the darkness itself, a towering figure with hair covering its head and an otherworldly aura that cooled the air around it materialized.

Meeting the Enigma: A Silent Exchange

The moment the campers and the mysterious figure locked eyes stopped time in its tracks; it was beyond description and transcended all language. The creature, also known as a Bigfoot, guarded the wilderness like a sentry and appeared to be both primordial and out of place. Its presence bridged the chasm between the unseen world that lay beyond and the human sphere with a weight that hinted at mysteries still unknown.

The beast and the campers stood together in mutual observation for an eternity. The campers were in amazement and unease as the creature quickly vanished back into the darkness after making an appearance. The encounter had cast a spell, causing concerns to arise that were beyond the range of accepted science.

Legacy of the Encounter: Echoes Through Time

The 2000 Green Swamp Encounter developed into a crucial thread in the elaborate web of Bigfoot legend. The campers' narrative supported the idea that these enigmatic beings might exist outside of the legendary forests of the Pacific Northwest because of its immediacy and the raw intensity of their experience. It served as a reminder that mysteries might establish themselves and flourish even amid the ostensibly familiar settings of the Southeast of the United States.

The meeting developed over time into more than just a personal account; it grew to symbolize the unexplored realms that continue to exist on the periphery of human comprehension. The Green Swamp, with its murky depths and whispered mysteries, continued to be a haven for enigmas; it was a place where the shadows held more than just gloom and where those who were prepared to travel deep into the forest could learn about the unseen.

Famous Bigfoot Sightings and Encounters cont'd

Legend of the Boggy Creek (Fouke Monster) (1971)

A sense of intrigue pervaded the dark, isolated woodlands of Fouke, Arkansas, where the humid, southern air hung thick. In 1971, a rural town was set to become well-known due to a string of bizarre and horrific occurrences. The circumstances that occurred permanently etched the term "Fouke Monster" into the annals of cryptozoological lore.

Fouke was a location where time appeared to move a little more slowly, where tales were handed down through the centuries like priceless relics, nestled among the cypress trees and swamplands. The locals had long whispered in secret about a mysterious creature that was rumoured to prowl the thickets and neighbouring bogs. However, it wasn't until the summer of 1971 that these legends would come to light.

As the story goes, a local family, the Fords, were the first to have a direct encounter with the enigmatic creature. Bobby and Elizabeth Ford's tranquil farmhouse stood as a silent sentinel on the outskirts of town. It was there, in the twilight hours, that their calm existence would be irrevocably disrupted.

Late one evening, the Fords were startled by an unsettling commotion outside. The dogs were barking with a ferocity that suggested something unnatural was lurking nearby. As Bobby stepped onto the porch, flashlight in hand, he was met with a sight that would forever haunt his dreams. A monstrous figure, covered in hair and standing at a height that seemed almost otherworldly, lumbered through the underbrush. Its eyes glowed with an eerie, reflective light, and its stench carried on the wind, a mixture of damp earth and something wholly primal.

The Fords were terrified as they watched the creature flee into the shadows, taking with it just the weight of their newly discovered fear and the echos of their racing hearts.

The Ford family's experience in Fouke quickly inspired other locals to share their own accounts of fleeting glances, unsettling sounds, and mysterious footsteps. Those who thought something strange was hiding in the shadows outnumbered the skeptics.

The Fouke Monster quickly gained notoriety outside of the town after a local newspaper picked up the tale. Widespread reports of sightings drew curious people, amateur sleuths, and skeptics seeking to learn the truth. Experts and fans flocked to the area and set up camp in an effort to gather proof.

In the middle of this upheaval, a director by the name of Charles B. Pierce recognized a chance to immortalize the legend on film. He used dramatic reenactments, eyewitness tales, and unsettling nocturnal images to create the docudrama "The Legend of Boggy Creek." When it was released in 1972, the movie connected with viewers, making the Fouke Monster a symbol of popular culture.

Years have passed since those turbulent summers of 1971, yet the Fouke Monster's legacy endures. With festivals, museums, and an unwavering sense of pride in its distinctive history, the town of Fouke has embraced its status as the creature's home.

A reminder that even in the modern world, there are mysteries that refuse to be fully solved and places where the unknown still holds sway, the legend of the Fouke Monster remains woven into the very fabric of the community as the sun sets over the cypress-studded landscape and the sounds of cicadas fill the air.

Famous Bigfoot Sightings and Encounters cont'd

The Haunting Encounter - Unraveling the Bauman Story

A narrative of terrifying intrigue—an encounter that combined fact and mystery—emerged among the immense expanse of the untamed American wilderness, where the lines between man and nature began to blur. Young Theodore Roosevelt set off on a hunting journey in the wide region of Montana in 1871, where he was doomed to witness a story that would live on in his memory forever.

Superstition was uncommon among the brave frontiersmen who travelled through these harsh environments because they lived lives of stern practicality. But one of them, a skilled mountain hunter by the name of Bauman, told Roosevelt a story that went against the grain of stoic reason. Roosevelt could not help but admit the reality of Bauman's account, despite its overtly frightful overtones and supernatural undertones.

Bauman had German roots, and stories of ghosts and goblins had been a big part of his youth. These early influences made him receptive to the mysterious, which later circumstances would accentuate. Bauman's tale started to take shape in the midst of Montana's rugged mountains.
Bauman set out on a hunting expedition with a friend, attracted to a remote pass where it was said to be teaming with beavers. The region had a bad reputation because the

previous year, rumours about a lone hunter's inexplicable death within its boundaries had spread. However, despite being aware of the numerous risks in the woods, Bauman was not deterred by the spectre of peril.

They set a camp and then ventured into the woods to set Beaver traps, navigating through the tangled undergrowth. They arrived back to camp as twilight was falling only to discover their hideaway disturbed. Darkness was kept at bay by campfires, which also created dancing shadows across the trees. However, what the campfire revealed was anything but comforting—their campground had been trashed, perhaps by a threatening presence. This unwanted visitor had destroyed their home, torn through their belongings, and caused mayhem. What they had thought at first to be a bear's prank took a disturbing turn.

Initial amazement gave way to anxiety when Bauman's companion examined the prints left behind. There were two distinct sets of paw prints, which seemed to contradict the laws of nature. Two-legged tracks sparked a sense of dread in a world where four-legged creatures were expected to govern. Bauman's worry grew as the night wore on, and the echoes of the forest took on a different resonance.

An encounter around midnight broke the silence. His senses abruptly alerted Bauman to a presence he couldn't see but was certain to feel. A persistent wild animal odour served as a sensory alert that danger was nearby. At the outskirts of the camp, a hulking figure lurked in the shadows. Bauman fired at the shadow. The spectre ran into the pitch-black depths of the woodland despite the gunshot from Bauman breaking the silence. A lingering scent of primordial evilness followed it.

Daybreak brought with it the sombre awareness that Bauman's story was far from over. Once more in chaos, their camp was evidence of the creature's erratic path of devastation. The footprints left behind, now indelible in the ground, offered a strange tale that defied interpretation. The monster appeared to be moving forward on two legs, a baffling revelation in the realm of rationality.

The two men were plagued by fear as its grip tightened. The odd shouts and rustlings coming from the shadows that had once been allies broke into the forest's evening symphony. Bauman felt more and more uneasy as time went on.

Bauman constantly felt like he was being watched while he gathered the traps. His partner had stayed behind to pack up and be ready to leave once Bauman returned. His paranoia increased as the line between the real and the imagined became hazy. It was

Bauman's conviction that the lurking presence was not of this world that solidified his resolve to depart the valley.

Their sensation of vulnerability was heightened by the solitude and emptiness of the valley. During Bauman's final trek through the gloomy woodland, which was defined by a pervasive fear, he came across a grizzly find. Once more, the camp lay in ruins, but this time, the uncomfortable truth was even darker. His partner's neck had been snapped and four unmistakable fang marks were on his throat, Bauman's partner was lying dead. The tracks were evidence of a predator from another world—a mystery monster.

Because of his terror, Bauman left the area quickly. Roosevelt took in Bauman's narrative, and his description of the terrifying experience became a monument to a man's brush with the unexplainable.

In the end, Roosevelt's story opens a window to a time when the unknown coexisted with the understood in the wilds. Despite being wrapped in superstition and terror, Bauman's meeting serves as a reminder of the thin line dividing the familiar from the enigmatic—a line that occasionally rises to expose secrets that surpass comprehension.

Famous Bigfoot Sightings and Encounters cont'd

Eric Shipton (1951) -Yeti footprints

When Mount Everest was still unaffected by the tourism that would eventually engulf it in the autumn of 1951, a party of daring English mountaineers set out on an important mission. They included Eric Shipton and Dr. Michael Ward, whose mission it was to map out probable routes to ascend Everest from Nepal. The results of this trip, under Shipton's direction, would provide the framework for Edmund Hillary and Tenzing Norgay's triumphant ascent two years later, which would be the first known successful ascent of Everest's heights. By establishing a route up the tallest mountain in the world, this expedition not only etched an important chapter in mountaineering history but also heralded a renaissance in climbing after the hiatus caused by World War II.

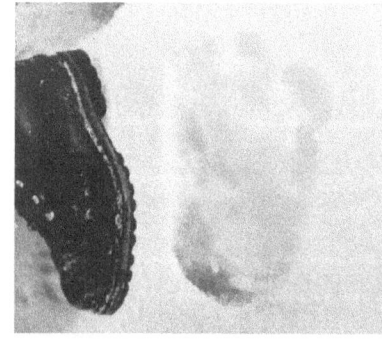

The 1951 trip, however, made history for a completely other cause. Shipton and Ward discovered a puzzling oddity in the Menlung Basin at an elevation of roughly 15,000 to 16,000 feet: a collection of mysterious footprints etched on the snow. They were forced to use whatever was available, including an ice pick, a knapsack, and Dr. Ward's left boot, as they lacked specific measuring equipment. Shipton captured every detail of the prints' discovery in a series of detailed images that he took of them. The unique breadth of the footprints—roughly twice that of a typical human foot, as Dr. Ward later determined—was revealed in one particular shot where a footprint was seen next to Dr. Ward's footwear. The big toe took on an abnormal prominence and placement, and the toe impressions appeared to be distorted. Was it possible that these footprints were even human? And if so, how had their makers navigated freezing snowscapes without footwear?

They followed the footprints down the glacier for a mile, puzzled yet intrigued, before setting up camp for the night. Days later, their teammates Tom Bourdillon and W. H. Murray joined them, lured by the intrigue of these unusual trails. Bourdillon's entry in his diary confirmed the startling and mysterious nature of this addition to their journey, even if the sun's glare had slightly warped the impressions by the time he arrived.

Shipton's photos sparked a flurry of interest upon their return to Britain. A swarm of cryptozoologists, monster aficionados, and mountaineers anxiously inspected the pictures and came to the same conclusion after each one: they had discovered proof of the fabled Himalayan Yeti.

The quest to prove the existence of the elusive Yeti drove a number of expeditions to the Himalayas and Central Asia as a result of this surge of fascination. But despite all of these combined efforts, not a single piece of tangible proof materialized. The very tracks that had sparked this occurrence were now the topic of doubt, with some speculating that Shipton had been a part of a large-scale con.

However, those who had shared the expedition's experience staunchly defended Shipton's integrity. Witnesses within their party corroborated the legitimacy of the photographs, bolstered by Bourdillon's own account in a letter he penned during the 1950s to Michael John Davies. In the end, Shipton's haunting images of those mystifying footprints served as a catalyst for a relentless quest into the unknown—an expedition for truth that mirrored their ascent of Everest, a climb against daunting odds, driven by curiosity and the unyielding human spirit.

Famous Bigfoot Sightings and Encounters cont'd

Australian Yowie-The Katoomba Incident

The Yowie is a mystical and elusive creature that is frequently compared to the Bigfoot of North America. It is the subject of one of the longest-lasting legends in Australian folklore. The Yowie has been the subject of reports for decades, capturing the interest of both locals and skeptics of the paranormal. One iconic experience stands out among the numerous recorded sightings as proof of the Yowie's mystique.

In the 1970s, an incident took place in the Blue Mountains of New South Wales, deep in the Australian outback, that would later become known as the Yowie sighting. The decision was made by a group of friends to go camping in a rural spot close to Katoomba. They had no idea that their excursion would result in a chilling encounter that defied explanation.

The mood was electric with anticipation and camaraderie as the group set up camp and settled in for the evening. Warmth and light were given by the bonfire, which also formed gyrating shadows on the trees in the area. As the companions savoured the peace of the wilderness, stories and laughter filled the air.

The peace was broken, though, by an ominous, guttural roar that shook the darkness. The anxious looks between the campers reflected the abrupt change in the atmosphere. They had never heard a roar like it before; it resonated with an almost primeval ferocity that gave them chills.

They concentrated on the tree line, where a huge figure stepped out of the darkness. The monster was towering at a commanding height and had a distinctly human shape. It loomed in the shadows of the bonfire, covered in hair and with a commanding presence. When the campers realized they were in the company of something both otherworldly and unquestionably real, their initial curiosity swiftly gave way to a primal horror.

The campers watched as the Yowie stayed outside of the campsite in a state of amazement and horror. Its guttural vocalizations seemed to ring with an otherworldly intent, and its eyes sparkled with an eerie knowledge. The moment the Yowie and the campers met eyes, it seemed as though time itself was holding its breath.

The campers struggled with the sense that they were walking in the unknown as the standoff went on for what seemed like an eternity. After then, the Yowie vanished into the night just as quickly as it had appeared, retreating back into the darkness.

The campers were left in a state of shock, grappling with the reality of what they had just witnessed. Their encounter with the Yowie had ignited a flame of curiosity, sparking a determination to uncover the truth behind the legends that had permeated their culture for generations.

This classic Yowie sighting in the Blue Mountains stands as a testament to the enduring allure of the unknown and the profound impact that unexplained phenomena can have on those who experience them. The encounter left an indelible mark on those campers, reminding them that even in the modern age, mysteries can still emerge from the depths of the wilderness, weaving their stories into the fabric of our understanding.

Chapter 6

Well known vocalizations:

The "**Ohio Howl**": This is a vocalization that was recorded in 1994 in Ohio and is considered by some researchers to be one of the most convincing pieces of evidence for Bigfoot's existence. The vocalization is a long, haunting howl that has been compared to a wolf's howl but is much louder and deeper.

The "**Sierra Sounds**": This is a collection of vocalizations that were recorded in the 1970s in the Sierra Nevada mountains of California. The recordings include a range of vocalizations, including whistles, grunts, and howls. Some researchers believe that the vocalizations represent a language or communication system used by Bigfoot.

The "**Crybaby Creek**" vocalizations: These are a series of vocalizations that were recorded in the early 2000s in the Pacific Northwest. The vocalizations include a range of sounds, including screams, growls, and whistles. Some researchers have suggested that the vocalizations represent Bigfoot calls for help or distress signals.

The "**Samurai Chatter**": This is a vocalization that was recorded in 1978 in Washington State. The vocalization has been described as a rapid, chattering sound that resembles a human voice speaking in an unknown language. Some researchers have suggested that the vocalization may be a form of Bigfoot communication.

The "**Ohio Moan**": This is a vocalization that was recorded in Ohio in 1981. The vocalization is a deep, guttural moan that has been compared to the sound of a large primate. Some researchers have suggested that the vocalization may be a territorial call or a mating call.

The "**Whoop-Howls**": This is a type of vocalization that has been reported in various parts of North America, including the Pacific Northwest and the Appalachian Mountains. The vocalization is a combination of a whoop and a howl and is often heard in the early morning or late evening. Some researchers have suggested that the vocalization may be a form of Bigfoot communication or a territorial call.

The "**Ohio 'Screams'**": This is a series of vocalizations that were recorded in Ohio in the 1980s and 1990s. The vocalizations are high-pitched screams that have been described as sounding like a woman or child in distress. Some researchers have suggested that the vocalizations may be produced by juvenile Bigfoot or may be used to lure prey.

The "**Puyallup Screamer**": This is a vocalization that was recorded in Washington State in the 1970s. The vocalization is a loud, high-pitched scream that has been compared to the sound of a woman screaming. Some researchers have suggested that the vocalization may be a warning call or an alarm signal.

The "**Sierra Samurai**": This is a vocalization that was recorded in the Sierra Nevada mountains in the 1970s. The vocalization is a series of rapid, staccato sounds that have been described as sounding like a Japanese samurai sword being unsheathed. Some researchers have suggested that the vocalization may be a form of Bigfoot communication or a warning signal.

The "**Gifting Howls**": This is a type of vocalization that has been reported in various parts of North America, including the Pacific Northwest and the Appalachian Mountains. The vocalization is a combination of a howl and a whistle and is often heard in response to gifts or offerings left for Bigfoot. Some researchers have suggested that the vocalization may be a form of gratitude or acknowledgement.

Chapter 7

How Natives describe Bigfoot.

Sasquatch: (Pacific Northwest): The legends of the Sasquatch are prevalent among tribes in the Pacific Northwest, such as the Coast Salish, **Kwakwaka'wakw**, and **Nuu-chah-nulth**. The Sasquatch is often depicted as a benevolent and mystical creature, possessing great wisdom and knowledge.

Skookum: (Chinook): Among the Chinook tribes of the Pacific Northwest, the Skookum is a term used to describe a powerful, wild man of the woods. The Skookum is believed to be both protective and elusive.

Omah: (Sioux): In Sioux folklore, the Omah is a giant, hairy creature that dwells in the forests and is known to be a keeper of the woods.

Yowie: (Aboriginal Australians): The Yowie is Australia's version of Bigfoot, according to Aboriginal Australian legends. It is often depicted as a large, hairy, and mysterious being roaming the wilderness.

Wendigo: (Algonquian): The Wendigo is a malevolent creature in Algonquian folklore, known to be cannibalistic and associated with the winter and starvation. Some believe it may have influenced aspects of Bigfoot mythology.

Yeti: (Himalayas): The Yeti, also known as the Abominable Snowman, is a mythical creature in Himalayan folklore. It is described as an ape-like being inhabiting the high mountain ranges.

Mapinguari: (Amazon Rainforest): In Amazonian folklore, the Mapinguari is a creature described as a giant sloth-like being with backward-facing feet. Some interpretations draw parallels with Bigfoot.

Momo: (Missouri): The legend of Momo, short for "Missouri Monster," revolves around reported sightings of a large, hairy creature in Missouri, USA, reminiscent of Bigfoot.

Chapter 8

Bigfoot Hotspots and Habitats around the world

Bigfoot activity has been reported all across the world. The historical significance of these sites and the regularity of claimed sightings have attracted the attention of researchers and enthusiasts.

Pacific Northwest, USA

Bigfoot sightings are most common in the Pacific Northwest, especially in the states of Washington, Oregon, and Northern California. With its thick forests, rough terrain, and plethora of fauna, this region is a perfect home for an elusive creature like Bigfoot. Bluff Creek, California, was the site of the renowned Patterson-Gimlin video, which increased the area's attraction to Bigfoot investigators. (see Chapter 9)

Canadian Wilderness

Another popular location for reports of Bigfoot sightings and interactions is British Columbia, Canada. Bigfoot and other huge monsters have plenty of possibilities to stay concealed in British Columbia's vast and inaccessible environment. The province's mountainous areas and coastal rainforests make for the perfect home for a cryptid like Bigfoot.

Ohio Grassman and Eastern United States

There are many Bigfoot stories from the eastern United States, even though the Pacific Northwest gets most of the attention. There are regional varieties of the species found in states like Ohio, Kentucky, and West Virginia, including the "Grassman." These places have extensive forests, which suggests that Bigfoot may live there.

Florida Everglades

Researchers studying Bigfoot have also been interested in the Florida Everglades. This area's deep woodlands and wetlands provide a distinctive and difficult setting to explore. Although reports of Bigfoot sightings in Florida are fewer than in the Pacific Northwest, some enthusiasts think the state may be home to the species.

Himalayan Region and Yeti

The Yeti, often called the Abominable Snowman, are a localized form of the Bigfoot myth that originated outside of North America in the Himalayan region. Reports of sightings and encounters with this elusive species have been made in the highland regions of Tibet, Bhutan, and Nepal. See Asian hotspots

Russian Wilderness and Almasty

Stories about a related monster called the Almasty have long been a part of Russian folklore. There are a lot of uncharted areas in the Caucasus Mountains and the distant wilderness of Siberia where cryptids similar to the Almasty might be found. See Asian hotspots

Australia's Yowie

Yowies are the Australian equivalent of Bigfoot. Reports of Yowie sightings and tales have surfaced across the nation, especially in the deep forests of Queensland and New South Wales.

Indigenous Legends and Sacred Sites

It's important to consider Indigenous legends and sacred sites in addition to specific physical locations when undertaking study on Bigfoot. Similar monsters are described in long-standing myths and legends from many Indigenous nations. They are commonly referred to as "Wild Men" or "Hairy Giants." Part of ethical Bigfoot research is to respect these cultural perspectives and to solicit advice from Indigenous groups.

Chapter 9

North America Hotspots:

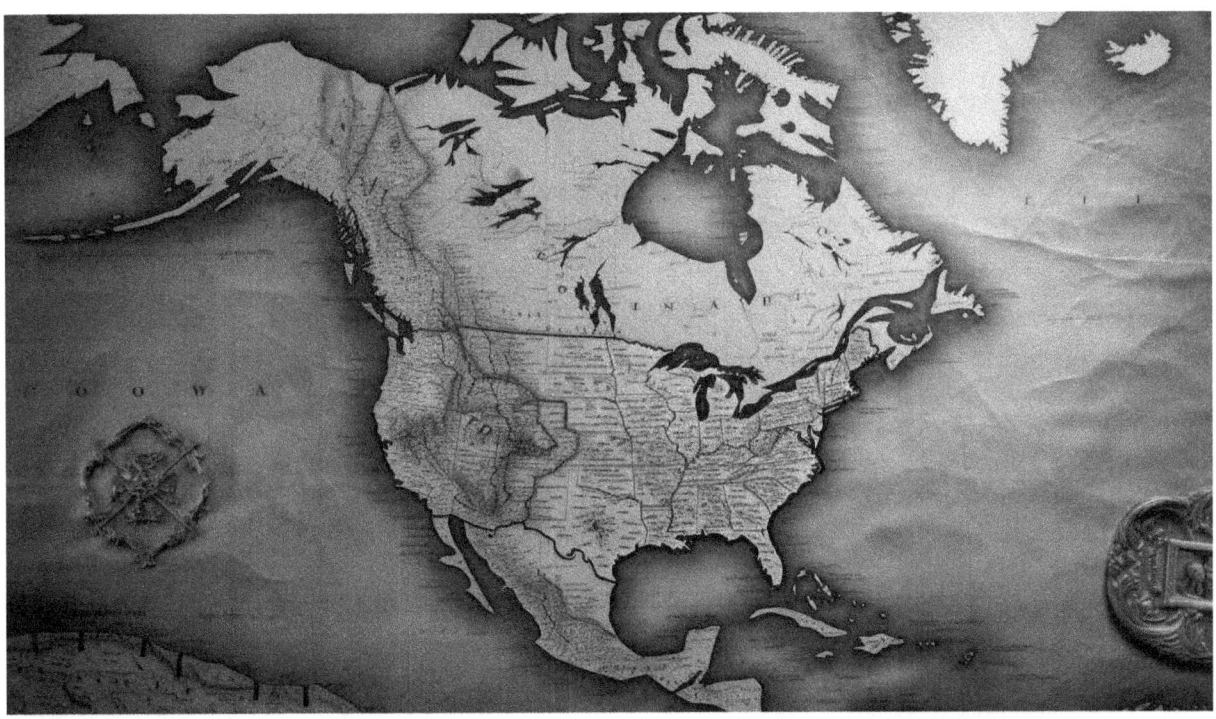

Bigfoot, popularly referred to as Sasquatch, is a fabled and elusive creature that resembles an ape in size and hair. Several sightings and interactions of Bigfoot have been reported around North America. Some locations have been identified as possible Bigfoot hotspots as a result of these reports. Here are some noteworthy examples:

Pacific Northwest (Washington, Oregon, Northern California)

- This region is perhaps the most famous hotspot for Bigfoot sightings. The dense forests and rugged terrain make it a suitable environment for an elusive creature to hide. The famous Patterson-Gimlin film, which is often cited as evidence of Bigfoot's existence, was filmed in Bluff Creek, California.

Cascade Mountains:

- The Cascade mountain range, which runs from northern California through Oregon and Washington, is known for its remote and heavily forested areas. There have been numerous Bigfoot sightings reported in these mountains over the years.

Olympic Peninsula (Washington):

- The Olympic Peninsula is another area known for its dense rainforests and isolated wilderness. It has a history of reported Bigfoot encounters and is home to the Olympic Project, a research group dedicated to studying the creature.

Sierra Nevada Mountains (California):

- The Sierra Nevada range is also a region where Bigfoot sightings have been reported. The combination of remote wilderness and large expanses of forested land provides potential habitats for such a creature.

Northern Rockies (Montana, Idaho):

The rugged terrain and extensive forests of the Northern Rockies offer potential hiding spots for elusive creatures like Bigfoot. Reports of sightings have come from this region as well.

British Columbia (Canada):

- This Canadian province has its own history of Bigfoot sightings and is often considered part of the overall Bigfoot phenomenon in the region.

Alberta(Canada):

- Many reported and investigated sightings from this province in Canada. Plenty of historical reports going back many years.

Ohio River Valley:

- Moving east, the Ohio River Valley has also seen a significant number of Bigfoot sightings over the years, particularly in states like Ohio, Kentucky, and West Virginia.

Florida Everglades:

- Even in the subtropical swamps of Florida, there have been reported sightings of a creature referred to as the "Skunk Ape," which is often considered a Southern variant of Bigfoot.

Chapter 10

Bigfoot Hotspots in Asia:

In this chapter, we'll look for potential Bigfoot hotspots in Asia. Numerous countries and regions on the vast and diverse Asian continent have reported sightings of large, hairy, secretive beasts resembling Bigfoot.

The Rich Folklore of Asia

Many legends and folktales about enigmatic and elusive monsters that closely resemble Bigfoot exist throughout Asia. In various civilizations, these animals are known by various names, including Yeti in the Himalayas, Yeren in China, Orang Pendek in Indonesia, and Almasty in the Caucasus.

The Himalayas and the Yeti

The Himalayas, stretching across countries like Nepal, Bhutan, and India, are renowned for their folklore about the Yeti or the Abominable Snowman. The Yeti is often described as a large, ape-like creature living in the snow-covered peaks of the Himalayas.

The Yeren of China

In China, the Yeren is said to be a wild, hairy hominid living in remote areas, particularly in the Hubei, Shaanxi, and Sichuan provinces. Sightings and reports of the Yeren have been part of Chinese folklore for centuries.

The Orang Pendek of Indonesia

In the dense forests of Sumatra, Indonesia, the Orang Pendek is believed to be a small, ape-like creature with human-like features. Locals and researchers have reported sightings and footprints attributed to this elusive creature.

The Almasty of the Caucasus

The Caucasus Mountains, stretching across countries like Russia, Georgia, and Azerbaijan, have their own legend of the Almasty, a hairy, ape-like creature living in the remote wilderness.

Chapter 11

Here are some steps you can take to get started if you're interested in becoming a Bigfoot researcher:

1. **Educate Yourself**: Start by studying the background, conjectures, and arguments around Bigfoot. Read the literature that is already available, both from supporters and opponents. You will gain a better understanding of the backdrop of your study and other points of view in the area.

2. **Stay Objective:** Keep an open mind and a healthy amount of skepticism as you conduct your study in order to remain objective. Remember that the burden of proof rests with those making the claims, and extraordinary claims necessitate extraordinary evidence.

3. **Field investigation**: Take into account undertaking field investigations if you're serious about your Bigfoot research. This could entail investigating locations where sightings have been recorded, searching for tracks, gathering potential evidence like hair samples or scat, and installing game cameras. Learn how to identify the various kinds of animal tracks and tracking methods.

4. **Network with Other Researchers:** Connect with other researchers using social media to form a network of Bigfoot aficionados. Participate in Bigfoot-related conferences, seminars, and online forums. You can exchange ideas and gain knowledge from more seasoned scholars by networking.

5. **Record Your Results**: Keep thorough records of all your inquiries, including the dates, times, locations, and weather details, as well as any proof you gather. Systematically record your observations and research approaches.

6. **Use Scientific Methods:** Utilize scientific approaches when conducting your research. This entails systematically and impartially gathering data, formulating and testing hypotheses, and arriving at conclusions supported by data.

7. **Respect the Environment and Ethics**: When performing field research, be sure to show consideration for the species and the environment. Get the required permits for research in protected regions, and observe ethical standards when observing wildlife.

8. **Critical Thinking:** Strong critical thinking abilities should be developed. This will assist you in evaluating the facts, evaluating claims, and avoiding confirmation bias, which is the tendency to believe only that which confirms your preconceptions.

9. **Learn About Related Subjects**: Learn about subjects like anthropology, primatology, zoology, and evolutionary biology. Your perspective on the topic will be more well-rounded if you are familiar with these fields.

10. **Documentaries and other forms of media**: If you want to share your research with a larger audience, think about making documentaries, publishing articles, or launching a blog or YouTube channel. However, avoid presenting unsubstantiated claims as facts and be upfront about the speculative character of your research.

Chapter 12

Bigfoot Research Techniques and Strategies

We'll look at the many strategies and tactics employed by seasoned researchers and enthusiasts in their hunt for Bigfoot-related proof. Remember that locating Bigfoot necessitates a methodical technique, patience, and expertise. (see Chapter 14)

Field Research and Investigation

It is imperative to perform extensive research prior to heading out into the bush in search of Bigfoot. Learn about the area you intend to explore by reading up on historical narratives, encounter reports, and documented sightings. Examine these stories for trends and similarities to pinpoint possible hotspots where Bigfoot activity has been documented in the past. (see Chapter 9)

Gathering Witness Testimonies

Conducting interviews with witnesses who report seeing Bigfoot is an essential part of field study. Speak with eyewitnesses face-to-face to obtain in-depth descriptions of their experiences. It's crucial to conduct these interviews with respect and without passing judgment because some people might be reluctant to talk about their experiences for fear of being made fun of. (see Chapter 19)

Setting Up Trail Cameras

Trail cameras are useful tools for Bigfoot hunting because they can record or photograph wildlife in isolated locations, giving researchers important information about possible Bigfoot habitats. Place trail cameras in key places where there have been reports or discoveries of evidence of Bigfoot activity, such as tree markings or footprints. Make sure you routinely check and replace your memory cards and batteries. (see Chapter 25)

Audio Recording and Vocalizations

Whistles, taps on wood, and other enigmatic vocalizations are frequently linked to Bigfoot. Invest in high-quality audio recording devices and turn them on for the entire night to record any strange noises in the area. Subsequent analysis of these recordings will aid in distinguishing vocalizations associated with Bigfoot from those of recognized animals.

Nighttime Observations

Bigfoot sightings have frequently happened at night. Use thermal imaging cameras or night vision equipment to observe during the night from a secure position in order to increase the likelihood that you will spot any large, bipedal animals moving through the shadows.

Tracking and Identifying Footprints

Bigfoot is renowned for leaving unusually shaped and sized footprints behind. Acquire the ability to recognize and distinguish authentic Bigfoot footprints from those of other creatures. When possible, cast footprints in plaster to preserve the evidence for future examination. (see Chapter 15,22)

Attractants and Baits

Certain places are targeted by some researchers using baits and attractants to get Bigfoot's attention. To attract the animal, food items such as nuts, fruit, or meat can be arranged in a strategic manner. But be cautious and don't use such methods to disturb the natural ecology or put animals at risk. (see Chapter 20)

Teamwork and Collaboration

A team approach is more successful when looking for Bigfoot. More thorough coverage of the field and cross-verification of results are made possible by collaborating with other seasoned researchers and enthusiasts. The general understanding of Bigfoot can also be improved by researchers exchanging information and materials with one another. (see Chapter 26)

Safety Precautions

When it comes to Bigfoot adventures, safety should always come first. Become familiar with the area's potential hazards and wilderness. To make sure you can call for assistance if necessary, let people know about your preparations and set up communication procedures. (see Chapter 17)

Chapter 13

Researchers Field Gear

The instruments you'll need to collect more significant evidence and advance your Bigfoot research are covered in this chapter. The right equipment, whether it be technical or field supplies, can increase the productivity and effectiveness of your research.

Field Gear

- Backpack: A sturdy and comfortable backpack is essential for carrying your research equipment, water, and other essentials during field investigations.
- Hiking Boots: Invest in a good pair of hiking boots with ankle support to navigate through rugged terrain.
- Weather-Appropriate Clothing: Dress in layers and wear weather-appropriate clothing to stay comfortable during varying conditions.
- Insect Repellent: Insect repellent can help protect you from bugs and ticks during your expeditions.

- Pocket Knife or Multi-Tool: A versatile tool like a pocket knife or multi-tool can come in handy for various tasks.
- Compass and GPS: Carry a compass and a GPS device to navigate through the wilderness accurately.
- Map: Always have a detailed map of the area you'll be exploring.
- Water and Food: Carry an adequate supply of water and non-perishable food items for your trip.
- First-Aid Kit: A well-stocked first-aid kit is essential for addressing minor injuries in the field.
- Field Notebook and Pens: Record your observations and findings in a field notebook.

Research Equipment

- Camera and Video Camera: A high-quality camera and video camera are vital for capturing evidence, including photos and videos of footprints, potential sightings, and the environment. (see Chapter 24)
- Binoculars or Spotting Scope: Binoculars or a spotting scope can help you observe distant objects or wildlife in greater detail.
- Trail Cameras: Set up trail cameras in potential Bigfoot hotspots to capture images or videos when you're not present. (see Chapter 25)
- Audio Recorder: Use an audio recorder to capture vocalizations or sounds in the woods.
- Thermometer: A thermometer can help measure temperature variations in potential Bigfoot activity areas.
- Night Vision and Thermal Imaging Devices: Night vision goggles or thermal imaging devices can improve nighttime observation capabilities.
- Plaster for Casting Footprints: Carry plaster or similar casting material for creating track castings. (see Chapter 15)
- Measuring Tape or Ruler: Use a measuring tape or ruler to document the size of footprints and other evidence.

Communication Equipment

- Two-Way Radios: Use two-way radios to maintain communication with your research team during field investigations.
- Satellite Phone: In remote areas with no cell service, a satellite phone can be a reliable means of communication in case of emergencies.

Technology and Analysis

- Laptop or Tablet: A laptop or tablet can be useful for reviewing and organizing evidence and data during your research.
- Mapping Software: Use mapping software to mark and track your research locations. (see Chapter 32)
- Image and Audio Analysis Software: Utilize image and audio analysis software to examine and enhance captured evidence.

Chapter 14

Tracking and Field Techniques

As we journey through this chapter, we embark on an exploration of the skills and mindset required to traverse the untamed realms where Bigfoot supposedly roams. By understanding the art of tracking and employing field techniques, we inch closer to the secrets that lie hidden within the natural world.

The Essence of Tracking

Tracking is both an ancient art and a modern science. The intuitive connection between tracker and trail, the ability to read the signs left behind by a creature, and the patience to piece together a story from the marks on the ground are fundamental aspects of tracking. This section introduces the essence of tracking and its significance in Bigfoot research.

Understanding Wildlife Signs

The wilderness is a canvas painted with the traces of its inhabitants. Learning to differentiate between tracks, scat, scratches on trees, broken vegetation, and other signs provides insights into the inhabitants of the area. By honing the skill of interpreting these signs, trackers can discern potential Bigfoot activity from the myriad of wildlife movements.

Navigating Terrain and Habitat

Bigfoot is rumoured to inhabit a diverse range of landscapes, from dense forests to remote mountains. This section discusses how field researchers must adapt their tracking techniques to suit varying terrains and habitats. The interplay between knowledge of ecosystems and tracking expertise is essential for successful fieldwork.

The Art of Observation

At the heart of tracking lies the art of observation. Trained eyes recognize patterns in the landscape and irregularities that hint at hidden movement. Learning to observe without preconceived notions is critical to distinguishing genuine evidence from the noise of the wilderness.

Footprints and Gait Analysis

Footprints, if authentic, can provide invaluable information about Bigfoot's size, stride, and gait. This section delves into the intricacies of analyzing footprints, measuring dimensions, and using forensic techniques to determine authenticity. Understanding how a creature moves through its environment can offer insights into its behaviour and habits.

Photographic Documentation and Scale

Field researchers often rely on photographs to document findings. Learning to photograph tracks, scat, and other evidence with a sense of scale is essential for analysis. The inclusion of a reference object, such as a ruler or a common item, aids in accurate measurement and verification.

Pattern Recognition and Behaviour Analysis

As trackers, researchers aim to decipher patterns in the landscape that indicate Bigfoot movement or activity. This requires the ability to differentiate between natural phenomena and potential evidence. Analyzing behaviour patterns, such as nesting sites or feeding areas, contributes to a deeper understanding of the creature's behaviour.

Casting and Preservation

When encountering particularly detailed or unique footprints, researchers may choose to create casts for preservation and analysis. The next chapter discusses the casting process, including materials and techniques, and highlights the importance of proper documentation to prevent contamination of the original evidence.

Chapter 15

Track Casting in Bigfoot Research

Bigfoot research uses the technique of "track casting" to preserve and study tracks found in the field. Researchers may reproduce footprints in exquisite detail via track casting, which aids further investigation and documentation.

The Importance of Track Casting

Footprints are one of the most significant pieces of evidence in Bigfoot research. Track casting is essential because it allows researchers to preserve the physical evidence left behind by the creature and study it in detail.

By creating castings of footprints, researchers can:

- Examine the dimensions of the print, such as length, width, and depth.
- Observe the number of toes and the arrangement of the toes in the print.
- Analyze the potential dermal ridges or skin impressions present in the print.
- Measure the stride length and gait pattern to estimate the creature's size and locomotion.
- Compare the castings to known animal prints to rule out misidentifications.

Materials Needed for Track Casting

To create a track casting, you will need the following materials:

- Plaster of Paris or a similar casting material: Plaster is commonly used for track casting due to its ease of use and availability. It can be purchased from most art or craft stores.
- Water: To mix with the plaster to create a workable casting mixture.
- Mixing container: A large, sturdy container to mix the plaster and water.
- Stirring stick: A stick or spatula for mixing the plaster.
- Plastic bags or cling film: To line the track and prevent the plaster from sticking to the ground.
- Shovel or trowel: To dig around the track and create a mold.

- Brushes: To clean debris and dirt from the track before casting.
- Water spray bottle: To moisten the track area and improve the casting result.
- Notepad and pen: To record details about the track before and after casting.

Steps for Track Casting

Follow these steps to create a track casting:

- Prepare the Area: Clean any debris or loose dirt from around the track using brushes. Moisten the track area slightly with the water spray bottle to improve the casting result.
- Create a Mold: Use a shovel or trowel to dig around the track, creating a mold that will contain the casting material.
- Line the Mold: Line the mold with plastic bags or cling film to prevent the plaster from sticking to the ground.
- Mix the Plaster: In the mixing container, combine the plaster with water following the manufacturer's instructions. Stir thoroughly until the mixture reaches a smooth consistency.
- Pour the Plaster: Carefully pour the plaster mixture into the mold, ensuring it covers the entire track.
- Tap the Mold: Gently tap the mold to release any air bubbles trapped in the plaster.
- Wait for the Plaster to Harden: Allow the plaster to dry and harden completely before removing the casting from the mold. This may take several hours.
- Document the Casting: Once the casting is hardened, remove it from the mold and carefully clean off any excess dirt or debris. Record details about the casting, such as the location, date, and any distinctive features observed.

Preserving and Transporting Castings

To preserve the casting for further analysis, store it in a dry and secure location. Avoid exposing the casting to excessive moisture or extreme temperatures, as these can damage the plaster.

When transporting the casting, ensure it is protected from any potential impact or damage. Wrapping the casting in bubble wrap or foam padding can help prevent it from breaking during transportation.

Remember, proper track casting is crucial for preserving the integrity of the footprint evidence and aiding in further research and analysis. Handle the castings with care and respect as you continue your investigation into the mysteries of Bigfoot.

Chapter 16

Field Audio Recording

Setting up audio recording equipment in the field for optimal results requires careful planning, attention to detail, and consideration of various factors. Whether you're recording wildlife sounds, natural ambiance, or potentially even cryptid vocalizations like those of Bigfoot or other mysterious creatures, here are some steps to help you achieve the best possible audio recordings:

Choose the Right Equipment:

Select high-quality recording equipment suited for field use. This typically includes a portable digital audio recorder or a high-end smartphone with a quality external microphone. Look for equipment with good low-noise characteristics and the ability to capture a wide frequency range.

Microphone Selection:

Choose an appropriate microphone for your intended recordings. For capturing wildlife sounds and natural ambiance, omnidirectional microphones are often preferred, as they pick up sounds from all directions. If you're targeting specific sounds, consider a directional microphone to focus on the desired source.

Wind Protection:

Wind noise can be a significant issue, especially in outdoor environments. Use windshields or foam wind covers to minimize wind noise during recording. These accessories help prevent unwanted gusts from distorting your recordings.

Location Scouting:

Choose your recording location carefully. Scout the area in advance to identify potential sources of noise interference, such as roads, machinery, or other human activity. Look for secluded spots that are likely to have minimal background noise.

Time of Day:
Different times of day can yield unique sounds. Early morning and dusk are often ideal for capturing wildlife activity and natural ambiance. Avoid midday when the sun is high and human activity is more common.

Microphone Placement:

Experiment with microphone placement to find the best balance between capturing the desired sounds and minimizing unwanted noise. Consider elevating the microphone to avoid capturing ground-level noises.

Recording Techniques:

Experiment with different recording techniques:

Ambient Recording: Set up the microphone in a central location and record the natural soundscape. This technique can provide a rich sonic environment.

Point-of-Interest Recording: Focus the microphone on a specific area or sound source, like a stream, bird's nest, or potential creature habitat.

Recording Levels:

Set recording levels conservatively to avoid clipping or distortion. Monitor your levels during recording to ensure that the audio remains clean and clear.

Test and Monitor:

Before starting a lengthy recording session, conduct test recordings to evaluate the quality and assess potential issues. Use headphones to monitor the recordings in real-time and make adjustments as needed.

Duration and Storage:

Record for extended periods to capture a variety of sounds, as the best moments might occur unexpectedly. Ensure you have sufficient storage space on your recording device or memory cards.

Quiet Intervals:

Allow for periods of silence between recordings. This can be helpful for later analysis, as it allows you to distinguish sounds and events more easily.

Post-Processing:

After recording, review your audio files on a computer to identify and mark any noteworthy sounds. You can also use audio editing software to enhance the recordings and reduce background noise if necessary.

Patience and Persistence:

The best outcomes frequently stem from persistence and patient work. Spend time in the field honing your skills and becoming familiar with the local noises.
Keep in mind that capturing vocalizations of enigmatic or elusive species, such as those attributed to cryptids, needs open-mindedness and a critical mindset. To give your recordings context, record your procedures, your surroundings, and the circumstances. Your recordings can help us comprehend the natural world, whether you're recording the recognized sounds of animals or perhaps discovering something new.

Chapter 17

Safety of Bigfoot Researchers

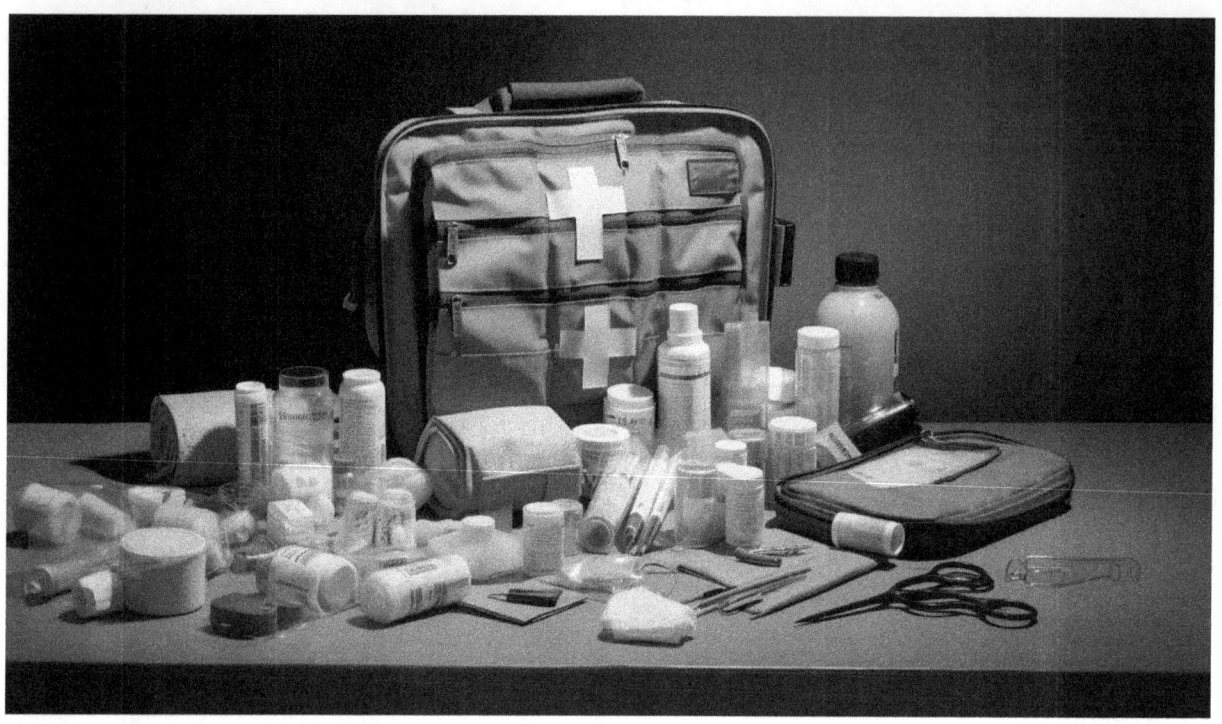

The focus of this chapter will be field investigation safety, providing researchers and enthusiasts embarking on Bigfoot expeditions with essential guidance and instructions. Even though the setting can be both challenging and thrilling, it is vital to ensure your safety.

Preparing for the Expedition

Before heading into the woods, take the following safety precautions:

- Research the Area: Familiarize yourself with the location you plan to explore, including potential hazards, wildlife, weather conditions, and local regulations.
- Share Your Itinerary: Inform a reliable person about your expedition plans, including the area you'll be exploring, the duration of your trip, and when you expect to return.
- Obtain Necessary Permits: If required, obtain any necessary permits or permissions for your research activities.

- Pack Essential Gear: Ensure you have appropriate camping equipment, first-aid supplies, navigation tools, communication devices, and enough food and water for the duration of your trip.

Navigation and Orientation

In the wilderness, proper navigation is vital. Follow these navigation tips:

- Carry a Map and Compass: Always have a detailed map of the area and a reliable compass to help you navigate.
- Learn Basic Navigation Skills: Familiarize yourself with basic navigation techniques, such as reading a map, using a compass, and understanding topography.
- Mark Your Starting Point: Before venturing into the woods, mark your starting point on the map to help you find your way back.
- Stay on Marked Trails: Stick to marked trails whenever possible, as they provide safer paths through the wilderness.

Wildlife Awareness

Encountering wildlife is a possibility in the woods. Here are some tips for wildlife safety:

- Keep a Safe Distance: Observe wildlife from a safe distance, and never approach or corner animals.
- Store Food Properly: Keep your food securely stored to prevent attracting wildlife to your campsite.
- Learn About Local Wildlife: Research the wildlife that inhabits the area you'll be exploring, including potential dangers and how to respond to encounters.

Weather Preparedness

Weather conditions in the wilderness can be unpredictable. Be prepared for various weather scenarios:

- Check the Forecast: Before your trip, check the weather forecast for the area you'll be exploring.
- Dress Appropriately: Wear weather-appropriate clothing, including layers to adjust to temperature changes.
- Seek Shelter if Needed: In case of adverse weather conditions, find shelter to stay safe and dry.

First Aid and Emergency Preparedness

Always be prepared for emergencies and potential injuries:

- Carry a First-Aid Kit: Have a well-stocked first-aid kit with essential medical supplies.
- Know Basic First Aid: Familiarize yourself with basic first-aid procedures to address minor injuries.
- Have a Communication Plan: Bring a reliable communication device, such as a satellite phone or two-way radio, in case of emergencies.
- Know Emergency Protocols: Be aware of local emergency protocols and how to reach help if needed.

Group Safety and Buddy System

If possible, conduct research in groups and use the buddy system:

- Stick Together: Stay close to your group members during expeditions.
- Buddy System: Assign each member a buddy, and regularly check on each other's well-being.

Leave No Trace

Respect the environment by adhering to the principles of "Leave No Trace":

- Pack Out Your Trash: Bring back all trash and waste with you, leaving no litter behind.
- Avoid Damage to Flora and Fauna: Avoid damaging plants or disturbing wildlife during your research activities.

Setting safety first can help you get the most out of your Bigfoot research experience and make sure that your outdoor adventure is risk-free, entertaining, and enlightening.

Chapter 18

What information should be recorded in field notes.

Field notes are essential for documenting observations and data collected during your research in the field. Well-organized and detailed field notes provide valuable information for analysis, comparison, and sharing your findings with others. Here are some key pieces of information that should be recorded in field notes:

- Date and Time: Record the date and time of each observation or encounter. This information is crucial for understanding patterns and correlations in your data.
- Location: Note the precise location of your research site using GPS coordinates or detailed descriptions of landmarks, trails, or geographical features.
- Weather Conditions: Record the weather conditions during your fieldwork, including temperature, humidity, precipitation, wind speed, and visibility. Weather can impact animal behaviour and evidence preservation.
- Research Objectives: Clearly state the goals and objectives of your research session. What are you specifically looking for, and what do you hope to accomplish?
- Observations: Describe your observations in detail. Note the behaviour of any animals encountered, including potential Bigfoot sightings, vocalizations, or other relevant activities.

- Environmental Features: Record details about the surrounding environment, such as the type of vegetation, water sources, elevation, and geological features.
- Encounter Circumstances: If you have any encounters with potential Bigfoot or witnesses, document the circumstances, including the number of individuals involved, their behaviour, and their responses.
- Physical Evidence: Describe any physical evidence you encounter, such as footprints, hair samples, tree structures, or any other potential signs of Bigfoot activity.
- Equipment Used: Note the equipment you used during the research session, including camera models, audio recorders, GPS devices, and any other relevant tools.
- Team Members: If you are working with a team, record the names and roles of each team member involved in the research.
- Sketches or Diagrams: Consider including sketches or diagrams to illustrate specific details, such as footprints or the layout of your research site.
- Field Conditions: Describe any challenges or unique conditions you faced during the fieldwork, such as difficult terrain, equipment malfunctions, or wildlife disturbances.
- Emotions and Impressions: Record your own emotions, impressions, and thoughts during the research session. This can add context to your observations and reflections on the experience.
- Potential Explanations: If you come across alternative explanations for your observations, note them in your field notes for later consideration and investigation.
- Safety Notes: Ensure you include safety-related information, such as any hazards encountered or precautions taken during the research.

Maintaining clear, accurate, and detailed field notes is essential for maintaining the integrity of your research and supporting the scientific process. Well-documented field notes enable transparency, facilitate analysis, and contribute to the credibility of your findings.

Chapter 19

Witness Interview Procedures in Bigfoot Research

In this chapter, we will delve into witness interview procedures, a critical aspect of Bigfoot research. Gathering detailed and accurate information from witnesses is essential for understanding their encounters and adding valuable data to your research.

The Importance of Witness Interviews

Witness interviews are crucial in Bigfoot research for several reasons:

- Firsthand Accounts: Witnesses provide direct, firsthand accounts of their experiences, offering valuable insights into potential Bigfoot sightings or encounters.
- Additional Information: Interviews can yield additional details such as the location, date, time, weather conditions, and behavior of the observed creature.
- Corroboration: Interviewing multiple witnesses from the same area can help corroborate their stories and strengthen the credibility of reported sightings.
- Contextualization: Understanding the witnesses' backgrounds, knowledge of the local wildlife, and cultural beliefs can provide context to their experiences.

Conducting Witness Interviews

When conducting witness interviews, keep the following guidelines in mind:

- Approach with Sensitivity: Witnesses may have had profound and sometimes frightening experiences. Approach the interview with empathy and understanding.
- Create a Comfortable Environment: Choose a private and comfortable location for the interview, where the witness feels at ease.
- Obtain Consent: Always seek the witness's consent to conduct the interview, and explain the purpose and significance of their contribution to the research.
- Build Rapport: Establish a rapport with the witness by engaging in casual conversation before delving into the details of their encounter. This can help build trust and make the witness feel more at ease.
- Ask Open-Ended Questions: Encourage witnesses to provide detailed accounts by asking open-ended questions, such as "Can you describe what you saw?" or "Tell me about the creature's appearance and behaviour."
- Record the Interview: With the witness's permission, audio or video record the interview to ensure accurate documentation. Alternatively, take detailed written notes during the interview.
- Avoid Leading Questions: Refrain from asking leading questions that might influence the witness's responses. Allow them to recount their experiences in their own words.
- Use Sketches or Maps: If possible, have witnesses draw sketches of the creature or the area where the sighting occurred. Maps can also help pinpoint the location.
- Inquire About Surroundings: Ask about the environment and terrain where the sighting took place, as well as any sounds or smells the witness may have noticed.
- Note Emotional Responses: Pay attention to the witness's emotional responses during the interview. Their emotional state can offer insights into the impact of the experience.
- Follow Up: If necessary, follow up with witnesses to clarify details or ask additional questions that may arise during your research.

Analyzing Witness Testimonies

Analyzing witness testimonies requires critical thinking and objectivity:

- Look for Consistency: Compare witness accounts for consistency in key details such as the creature's appearance, behaviour, and location of the sighting.

- Seek Collaboration: If possible, seek to corroborate witness accounts by interviewing multiple witnesses or analyzing evidence from the area.
- Consider Alternative Explanations: Be open to alternative explanations for the reported sightings, such as misidentifications of known animals or natural phenomena.
- Document and Preserve: Thoroughly document witness testimonies and store them securely as part of your research data.

By conducting careful and respectful witness interviews and analyzing their testimonies thoughtfully, you can contribute valuable data to the field of Bigfoot research.

Questions to Ask an Eyewitness

Before we begin, remember to approach the interview with empathy and sensitivity, as witnesses may have had profound and sometimes frightening experiences. Building rapport and creating a comfortable environment are essential to encourage witnesses to share their accounts openly.

General Information

- Can you please state your full name?
- How old are you?
- What is your occupation?
- How long have you lived in this area?
- Have you ever heard about or had any interest in Bigfoot or similar creatures before your encounter?
- Have you ever encountered anything similar to what you saw on this occasion?

Encounter Details

- Date and time of the encounter?
- Location of the sighting (include GPS coordinates if possible)?
- Were you alone during the encounter, or were others present with you?
- Can you describe the weather conditions at the time of the encounter?
- Were you engaged in any specific activities at the time of the sighting?
- How far away were you from the creature?
- What was the creature doing when you first noticed it?
- Did you make any attempts to approach or interact with the creature?
- How long did the encounter last?
- How did the creature react to your presence?
- Did you notice any vocalizations or sounds made by the creature?

- Were there any distinctive odors associated with the creature?
- Did you notice any tracks or footprints left by the creature?

Creature Description

- Can you describe the creature's appearance? (e.g., height, weight, hair color, facial features, etc.)
- Did you observe any specific anatomical features, such as arms, legs, hands, or feet?
- How would you describe the creature's overall build or physique?
- Did you notice any unusual characteristics or markings on the creature?
- What was the creature's behaviour like during the encounter?

Surroundings and Environment

- Can you describe the terrain and vegetation in the area where the sighting occurred?
- Were there any bodies of water or significant landmarks nearby?
- Were there other wildlife or animal sounds in the vicinity at the time of the encounter?

Emotional and Physical Impact

- How did you feel during the encounter? (e.g., scared, curious, excited, etc.)
- Have you experienced any emotional or psychological effects since the encounter?
- Did you experience any physical sensations during or after the encounter?

Follow-Up Questions

- Have you shared your encounter with anyone else? If so, what were their reactions?
- Have you heard of any similar encounters or stories from others in the area?
- Is there anything else you would like to add or mention about your encounter?

Never forget to pay close attention while you listen, and refrain from interjecting into a witness's testimony. Let them tell you about their experience in their own terms, but make sure you record their answers precisely.

By asking these questions and closely studying the witness's account, you may contribute significantly to the field of Bigfoot research and advance our understanding of this enigmatic species.

Chapter 20

What attracts a Bigfoot?

While there is no definitive answer to what might attract Bigfoot, some theories and anecdotal reports suggest the following factors:

- **Food Sources**: Bigfoot is often described as an omnivorous creature, and it is believed to be attracted to food sources such as berries, fruits, nuts, small animals, and fish. Researchers sometimes use bait stations with food items to potentially lure the creature.
- **Water Sources**: Like any wildlife, Bigfoot might be attracted to areas with easily accessible water sources, such as rivers, streams, and lakes.
- **Remote and Undisturbed Areas**: Bigfoot is commonly associated with wilderness and remote areas far from human activity. These creatures are often believed to avoid heavily populated regions.
- **Mating and Social Behavior**: During mating seasons, some researchers speculate that Bigfoot might be more active and possibly attracted to specific areas where potential mates are present.
- **Vocalizations and Calls**: Some researchers believe that Bigfoot uses vocalizations and calls to communicate, and mimicking these sounds might attract their attention.

- **Curiosity and Observation**: Some anecdotal reports suggest that Bigfoot might be curious about humans and could be attracted to areas where human activity is evident.
- **Weather Patterns**: Some researchers speculate that Bigfoot might follow seasonal weather patterns or move to areas with favorable climate conditions.
- **Energy Sources**: There are theories suggesting that Bigfoot might be attracted to sources of energy, such as electrical fields or magnetic anomalies such as hydro lines.

Chapter 21

What time of day are you most likely to encounter a Bigfoot or Bigfoot vocalization?

Reports of Bigfoot vocalizations and encounters with the creature are frequently anecdotal and very variable. It is difficult to pinpoint certain dates when encounters with Bigfoot are most likely to happen because there is no scientific proof of his existence. Nonetheless, various reports and speculations have led to the suggestion of the following patterns:

- **Nighttime**: Many Bigfoot sightings and vocalization reports have occurred during the nighttime. This is likely due to reduced human activity and increased animal movement during the nocturnal hours.
- **Dawn and Dusk**: Bigfoot sightings have been reported during the early morning (dawn) and late afternoon (dusk) hours. These times often coincide with periods of transition between daylight and darkness, which might offer favorable conditions for the creature to remain hidden while being active.

Where:

- **Quiet and Remote Locations**: Encounters and vocalizations are more likely to be reported in quiet and remote locations, away from human habitation and noisy areas.
- **Seasonal Variations**: Some researchers suggest that Bigfoot might be more active during certain seasons, such as spring and fall, when food sources are abundant, and weather conditions are favourable.
- **Proximity to Water Sources**: Reports suggest that Bigfoot might be attracted to water sources, so encounters might be more likely in areas near rivers, lakes, or streams.
- **Specific Habitats**: Bigfoot is often associated with dense forests, mountainous regions, and wilderness areas. Therefore, encounters might be more common in these types of habitats.

Chapter 22

Analyzing Evidence and Differentiating Bigfoot Signs

In this chapter, we'll look at evidence analysis skills and learn how to tell suspected Bigfoot signs from natural occurrences. It is essential to assess the evidence attentively in order to differentiate between real data and fabrications or misidentifications.

Footprint Analysis

Footprint evidence is among the most important pieces of evidence in Bigfoot study. The following characteristics should be noted when examining footprints:

- Size: Genuine Bigfoot prints are usually larger than those of known animals, with lengths ranging from 15 to 24 inches.
- Stride Length: Measure the distance between each footprint to determine the creature's stride. Bigfoot is believed to have a long stride due to its massive size.
- Toe Arrangement: Bigfoot footprints often display five toes, similar to human footprints. Look for any signs of dermal ridges or skin impressions.

- Depth: Genuine footprints may exhibit considerable depth due to the creature's weight.

Tree and Branch Markings

There are reports that Bigfoot communicates via wood knocks, tree constructions, and other tree markings. Seek out unusual formations that don't seem to belong in the surrounding landscape. Look out for any bent, twisted, or broken tree limbs that would indicate Bigfoot activity.

Vocalizations and Recordings

Bigfoot vocalizations on audio recordings can be difficult to evaluate, but the following traits may help you tell them apart from other sounds:

- Range: Bigfoot vocalizations often fall within a low-pitched range, resembling deep howls or growls.
- Duration: Genuine vocalizations might last longer than those of typical wildlife sounds.
- Patterns: Listen for repetitive or distinct patterns that are uncommon in known animals.

Photography and Video Analysis

Though they are easily altered or misconstrued, photographs and videos are nonetheless important types of evidence. While examining visual proof:

- Check for Clarity: Clear, high-resolution images are preferred, as blurry or low-quality pictures might not provide sufficient details.
- Observe Behaviour: Note the creature's behavior in videos or images to evaluate whether it aligns with known animal behaviour.

Hair and DNA Samples

Rarely, hair samples that are supposedly connected to Bigfoot have been gathered. If you come across any hair, get advice from specialists in DNA analysis and hair identification to find out if it belongs to an unidentified primate or matches a known species. (see Chapter 9)

Scat and Fecal Samples

If feces are discovered, they can reveal details on the physiology and diet of the animal. To exclude other animals with comparable diets, scat analysis must be done by specialists and calls for specific understanding.

Thermal Imaging and Night Vision

For the purpose of identifying heat signatures or movements in the dark, thermal imaging cameras and night vision equipment can be quite helpful. Learn how to use this equipment so that you don't mistake it for human activity or wildlife.

Skeptical Inquiry

While assessing the data, maintain an open mind but be skeptical. Before attributing signs to Bigfoot, take into account other possible explanations and rule out known species or natural phenomena.

Consulting Experts

Consult with authorities in pertinent disciplines, such as zoology, anthropology, cryptozoology, or primatology, where the evidence is equivocal. Working with specialists can give your research more credence.

Chapter 23

Best Practices for Setting Up Basecamp in the Wilderness

For field investigations to be safe and comfortable, a basecamp that is properly set up and organized is necessary.

Choosing the Right Location

Selecting the right location for your basecamp is crucial for a successful expedition. Consider the following factors when choosing a site:

- Proximity to Research Area: Choose a location close to the research area, minimizing travel time and effort to reach potential Bigfoot hotspots.
- Water Source: Camp near a reliable water source, such as a river, stream, or lake, for drinking, cooking, and washing purposes.
- Flat and Level Ground: Look for flat and level ground to set up tents and equipment, ensuring a comfortable and stable basecamp.
- Shelter from Elements: Seek natural shelter from wind, rain, and harsh weather conditions, or bring appropriate shelter such as tents or tarps.
- Wildlife Considerations: Avoid camping near potential wildlife hazards or in areas with a history of aggressive wildlife encounters.

- Safety and Accessibility: Choose a location that is easily accessible in case of emergencies and offers clear communication with the outside world if possible.

Setting Up Tents and Shelter

Ensure your shelter provides comfort and protection during your stay in the wilderness:

- Tent Selection: Choose durable and weather-resistant tents that accommodate the number of researchers in your team.
- Proper Tent Pitching: Follow the manufacturer's instructions for setting up tents correctly to ensure stability and protection from the elements.
- Ground Preparation: Clear any debris or sharp objects from the tent area and consider using a groundsheet or footprint to protect the tent floor.
- Rainfly and Stakes: Use the rainfly to protect against rain and secure the tent with stakes to withstand wind.
- Campfire Safety: If allowed and necessary, set up a designated fire ring away from tents and combustible materials. Always follow local regulations and safety guidelines for campfires.

Organizing Basecamp

Keep your basecamp organized and efficient to facilitate your research activities:

- Cooking Area: Set up a designated cooking area away from tents to avoid food odors attracting wildlife.
- Food Storage: Use bear-proof containers or hang food in trees to prevent wildlife from accessing it.
- Trash Management: Bring trash bags and pack out all waste. Leave no trace of your presence in the wilderness.
- Equipment Storage: Keep research equipment organized and protected from weather conditions.
- Camp Hygiene: Practice good hygiene, including regular hand washing and proper waste disposal.

Safety and Security

Prioritize safety and security during your time at basecamp:

- Wildlife Awareness: Be aware of wildlife in the area and take appropriate precautions to avoid encounters.
- First Aid Kit: Have a well-stocked first aid kit readily available in case of injuries.

- Emergency Communication: Carry communication devices such as satellite phones or radios to summon help if needed.
- Emergency Plan: Develop an emergency plan with your team, including a designated meeting point and communication protocol in case of separation.

Leave No Trace

Finally, adhere to Leave No Trace principles to minimize your impact on the wilderness:

- Respect Nature: Observe wildlife from a distance and avoid disturbing their habitats.
- Pack Out Trash: Take all waste, including food wrappers and toilet paper, back with you.
- Minimize Campfire Impact: Use existing fire rings or camp stoves for cooking.
- Stay on Designated Trails: Avoid trampling on vegetation and stick to designated trails whenever possible.

By following these best practices for setting up basecamp in the wilderness, you can create a safe, comfortable, and sustainable environment for your Bigfoot research expeditions.

Chapter 24

Using GoPro cameras or similar.

While conducting research on Bigfoot, using GoPro cameras or other similar cameras to record continuously can be a beneficial strategy. These sturdy, little cameras have a long recording time for high-quality video. When utilizing GoPro cameras to further investigate Bigfoot, bear the following benefits and factors in mind:

Benefits

- Continuous Recording: GoPro cameras can be set to record continuously for extended periods, allowing researchers to capture footage throughout the day and night without interruption.
- Wide-Angle Lens: GoPro cameras typically have wide-angle lenses, which can capture a broad field of view, increasing the chances of capturing potential Bigfoot activity.
- Weatherproof: GoPro cameras are designed to withstand various environmental conditions, making them suitable for outdoor research, even in challenging weather.

- Versatility: GoPro cameras can be mounted on various surfaces, including trees, poles, and structures, allowing researchers to position them strategically in potential Bigfoot hotspots.
- Night Vision: Some GoPro models have night vision capabilities, which can be useful for recording in low-light conditions or during nighttime investigations.
- Remote Access: Many GoPro models offer remote access and live streaming features, allowing researchers to monitor and control the cameras from a distance.

Considerations:

- Battery Life: Continuous recording can drain the camera's battery quickly, so researchers need to ensure they have sufficient power sources or extra batteries to keep the cameras running.
- Data Storage: Continuous recording generates a large amount of data, so researchers should have ample storage capacity, such as high-capacity memory cards, to store the footage.
- Camera Placement: Proper camera placement is crucial to capturing potential Bigfoot activity effectively. Researchers should carefully choose locations with reported sightings or evidence to maximize the chances of recording relevant footage.
- Ethics and Regulations: Researchers must respect the environment, wildlife, and private property while deploying GoPro cameras. Ensure compliance with local laws and regulations regarding the use of cameras in public spaces and private properties.
- Analysis and Review: Analyzing hours of continuous footage can be time-consuming. Researchers need to allocate sufficient time for reviewing the recorded material carefully.
- False Positives: Continuous recording may capture unrelated wildlife or environmental activities, leading to false positives that require careful analysis and elimination.

Utilizing GoPro cameras to continuously capture film may be a helpful supplement to other methods used in Bigfoot research, such as audio recording, tracking footprints, and field observations. GoPro cameras, when utilized and cared for properly, can be a priceless tool in the ongoing quest to solve the mystery surrounding Bigfoot.

Chapter 25

How to Optimize Placement of Trail Cameras

In this chapter, we'll examine the best ways to strategically install trail cameras to maximize your chances of discovering potential Bigfoot evidence when doing research visits. Proper placement of your trail camera can improve your chances of capturing images or videos of this elusive animal.

Choose the Right Trail Camera

Before we dive into placement strategies, it's essential to select a trail camera suitable for your research needs. Consider the following factors:

- High Resolution: Choose a trail camera with high-resolution image and video capabilities to capture clear and detailed evidence.
- Infrared or No-Glow Technology: Opt for a trail camera with infrared or no-glow technology to avoid startling wildlife or potential Bigfoot activity.
- Battery Life: Select a trail camera with a long-lasting battery to ensure it remains operational for extended periods.
- Trigger Speed: Look for a trail camera with a fast trigger speed to capture quick movements effectively.

Key Trail Camera Placement Strategies

- Identify High-Probability Areas: Research historical Bigfoot sightings, reports, and potential habitat preferences to identify areas with a higher probability of Bigfoot activity.
- Cover Entrances and Exits: Place trail cameras at the entrances and exits of potential Bigfoot habitats, such as dense forests or secluded areas.
- Follow Game Trails: Position trail cameras along game trails, as Bigfoot may use these paths to move through the wilderness.
- Water Sources: Set up trail cameras near water sources, such as rivers, streams, or lakes, where Bigfoot might come to drink.
- Food Sources: If possible, monitor areas with potential food sources for Bigfoot, such as berry patches, fruit trees, or natural food caches.
- Survey Clearings and Open Spaces: Bigfoot might use clearings or open spaces for observation, hunting, or resting. Place trail cameras to monitor these areas.
- Height and Angle: Mount trail cameras at a height and angle that covers the potential movement and activity range of Bigfoot. Position the camera downward to capture footprints and other evidence on the ground.
- Multiple Cameras: Use multiple trail cameras to cover a wider area and capture different angles of potential Bigfoot activity.
- Concealment: Camouflage trail cameras to blend in with the surrounding environment, reducing the chances of detection by wildlife or humans.

Check and Maintain Trail Cameras

Regularly check and maintain your trail cameras to ensure they function optimally:

- Battery Replacement: Replace batteries as needed to prevent interruptions in camera operation.
- Memory Card Management: Clear and format memory cards before each expedition to maximize storage capacity.
- Regular Maintenance: Clean and inspect trail cameras for dirt, debris, or damage that may affect their performance.

Review and Analyze Trail Camera Footage

After retrieving the trail camera footage, review and analyze the images and videos carefully. Look for any potential Bigfoot evidence, such as footprints, distinctive creatures, or unexplained movements.

Share Findings and Collaborate

If you capture potential Bigfoot evidence on your trail cameras, share your findings with the Bigfoot research community or other researchers for analysis and verification. Collaboration with experts can provide valuable insights and contribute to the ongoing quest for evidence of Bigfoot. (see Chapter 26)

Chapter 26

Collaboration and Community in Bigfoot Research

Collaborating with colleagues, scholars, hobbyists, and local communities can significantly improve the advancement and legitimacy of your research.

Joining Research Groups and Organizations

To interact with the Bigfoot research community, joining reputable research groups and organizations is one of the best methods to do so. These associations offer a forum for interacting with seasoned researchers, exchanging insights, and taking part in collective fieldwork. Working together facilitates access to a wider variety of viewpoints and levels of experience, which results in deeper research.

Attending Conferences and Workshops

One of the best ways to engage with the Bigfoot research community is to become a member of credible research groups and organizations. These organizations provide a platform for engaging with experienced researchers, sharing knowledge, and participating in group fieldwork. Cooperation opens doors to a greater range of perspectives and expertise, leading to more in-depth study.

Sharing Findings and Data

Open communication and transparency are essential to Bigfoot research. Give the research community access to your data, facts, and conclusions so they can comment and analyze them. Working with others validates or improves your research and fosters constructive feedback.

Respecting Indigenous Knowledge

Many Indigenous communities have long-standing myths and beliefs about monsters that resemble Bigfoot. It is crucial to respect Indigenous people's knowledge and cultural viewpoints when conducting research in places where they live. Seek advice and cooperation from nearby communities, and handle the topic with tact and cultural understanding.

Citizen Science Initiatives

Engaging in citizen science programs can be a beneficial approach to support Bigfoot investigations. The public is urged by certain groups and researchers to record sightings, provide supporting documentation, or take part in data gathering activities. By including the public in the scientific process, these projects aid in the collection of a larger dataset.

Peer Review and Publication

If you think you have strong proof or important discoveries, you should think about publishing your work in peer-reviewed journals or other respected media. Peer review gives your work more legitimacy by guaranteeing that your findings are subjected to in-depth examination by subject matter experts.

Online Communities and Forums

Participate in Bigfoot research forums and groups online. These sites facilitate global enthusiast and researcher cooperation, knowledge exchange, and discussion. But be skeptical and use critical thinking when assessing material that is posted online.

Educational Outreach

Dispelling myths and misunderstandings concerning Bigfoot research and cryptozoology can be accomplished through public education. You may help to build a more serious and reputable field of study by encouraging responsible and evidence-based investigation.

Supporting Conservation Efforts

Research into Bigfoot usually entails time spent in wilderness and natural surroundings. Take part in conservation initiatives to save these ecosystems and the animals that live there. For Bigfoot study to be ethical, the natural environment must be respected and preserved.

Collaborating with others and actively engaging in the Bigfoot research community can help you contribute to the expanding and trustworthy collection of information about this elusive creature. Remember that finding conclusive evidence of Bigfoot's existence takes a team effort and numerous dedicated, cooperative individuals.

Chapter 27

Speaking to Authorities about Bigfoot Knowledge

Methods for approaching and conversing with relevant authorities or specialists about your Bigfoot investigation and discoveries. If you wish to establish credibility and maybe obtain their support for your research, you must interact with authorities in a responsible and polite manner.

Know Your Audience

Before approaching authorities, understand who they are and their level of knowledge or interest in Bigfoot research. Some authorities may have experience or familiarity with the subject, while others may be skeptical or uninformed. Tailor your communication approach accordingly.

Be Respectful and Professional

When speaking to authorities, maintain a respectful and professional demeanour. Approach them with courtesy and openness, even if they express skepticism or lack of interest. A professional attitude can positively influence their perception of you and your research.

Present Evidence and Data

Back up your claims and knowledge with tangible evidence and data. Provide any Bigfoot-related research findings, photographs, footprints, audio recordings, or other evidence you may have collected during your field expeditions. The more concrete evidence you can present, the more likely authorities may take your research seriously.

Share Your Research Goals

Clearly communicate your research goals and objectives. Explain your interest in Bigfoot research and the potential contributions it can make to the fields of wildlife biology, anthropology, and folklore. Highlight how your research aligns with broader scientific inquiry.

Address Safety Concerns

If authorities express concerns about safety during your research activities, address them responsibly. Discuss the safety protocols you follow, including communication devices, emergency plans, and wilderness training.

Discuss Collaboration and Information Sharing

Express your willingness to collaborate with authorities or other researchers who may have relevant expertise. Emphasize your commitment to responsible and ethical research practices and your interest in sharing information for the greater understanding of wildlife and wilderness.

Listen and Be Open-Minded

Listen to the perspectives of authorities and be open-minded to their viewpoints, even if they differ from your own. Engage in constructive discussions and be willing to learn from their experiences and knowledge.

Respect Privacy and Confidentiality

If authorities request confidentiality about certain information or discussions, respect their wishes. Confidentiality may be necessary for various reasons, such as ongoing investigations or protecting sensitive information.

Follow Local Regulations

Adhere to local regulations and laws when conducting your research. Obtain necessary permits or permissions, and be mindful of any restrictions on accessing certain areas.

Promote Education and Awareness

Lastly, use your interactions with authorities as an opportunity to promote education and awareness about Bigfoot and wildlife conservation. Encourage dialogue and interest in the natural world and the mysteries that it holds.
By politely, professionally, and with evidence in hand, you may contribute to a more educated and candid discussion on this intriguing issue by sharing your knowledge about Bigfoot with authorities.

Chapter 28

Theory on the Migration of Bigfoot

In this chapter, we shall explore the theory surrounding Bigfoot's potential migration routes. Owing to Bigfoot's elusive nature and the vast geographic variety of sightings documented, various scientists and enthusiasts have speculated on the creature's potential travel routes and dwelling places.

Widespread Distribution

Bigfoot sightings and encounters have been reported in various parts of the world, including North America, Asia, and other regions. This widespread distribution has sparked curiosity about how these creatures might travel and adapt to diverse environments.

Seasonal Migration

According to one notion, Bigfoot might migrate seasonally, just like a lot of other animal species. Certain scientists surmise that these organisms might migrate to other regions based on seasonal variations in weather or food availability.

Following Food Sources

Another hypothesis is that Bigfoot might migrate in search of food. Being omnivores, they could follow the movement of prey animals or seasonal food availability, much like other large predators.

Avoiding Human Activity

The reclusive nature of Bigfoot may lead them to move away from areas with high human activity. As urbanization and development encroach upon natural habitats, Bigfoot might be forced to migrate to more remote and less populated regions.

Adapting to Environment

Some researchers suggest that Bigfoot's ability to adapt to different environments could allow them to thrive in various regions, enabling them to move between different types of landscapes and habitats.

Corridors and Migration Routes

Just like many other animal species, Bigfoot might use natural corridors and migration routes to move between different areas. These corridors could include river valleys, mountain ranges, and other geographic features.

Dispersal of Populations

The theory of population dispersal proposes that Bigfoot populations might be spread out, and individual creatures could move to establish territories or find mates.

Avoiding Interactions with Humans

Because of their supposed intellect and survival instinct, bigfoots may migrate away from densely populated areas and avoid places where people are often present.

Chapter 29

Using Drones for Bigfoot Research

Investigate the possible uses of drones in Bigfoot research. Unmanned aerial vehicles (UAVs), sometimes referred to as drones, are becoming more and more common instruments for a variety of research and surveillance uses. In the realm of Bigfoot research, in particular, they can provide special benefits.

Aerial Surveying and Mapping

Drones equipped with high-resolution cameras can conduct aerial surveys and create detailed maps of the terrain, helping researchers identify potential Bigfoot habitats and conducting reconnaissance in hard-to-reach areas.

Aerial Surveillance

Drones equipped with thermal imaging cameras can be used for aerial surveillance, allowing researchers to scan large areas for heat signatures that might indicate the presence of a large, warm-blooded creature like Bigfoot.

Monitoring Wildlife Activity

Drones can be used to observe and monitor wildlife activity, including potential prey animals that Bigfoot might be attracted to, providing valuable insights into the creature's potential food sources.

Search and Rescue Operations

In cases where individuals might be lost in remote wilderness areas while conducting Bigfoot research, drones can aid in search and rescue operations, improving the safety and efficiency of rescue efforts.

Low Impact Research

Using drones for aerial observation reduces the need for researchers to physically enter sensitive habitats, minimizing disturbances to the environment and wildlife.

Remote Monitoring

Drones with live-streaming capabilities can transmit real-time data, enabling researchers to remotely monitor and assess potential Bigfoot activity.

Cost-Effectiveness

Compared to traditional manned aircraft or ground-based methods, drones are often more cost-effective, making them an accessible tool for researchers with limited resources.

Data Collection and Analysis

Drones can collect large amounts of data quickly, and researchers can analyze the information collected to identify patterns or anomalies that may be associated with Bigfoot presence.

Collaboration with Ground Teams

Drones can work together with on-the-ground research teams to provide new perspectives and improve coordination.
Although using drones for Bigfoot research has numerous advantages, it's vital to consider the limitations and ethical implications. Researchers must respect people's privacy and safety when utilizing drones, be aware of local laws governing their use,

and take into account any potential negative effects their actions may have on the environment and wildlife.

Chapter 30

Collecting DNA samples in the field

Collecting DNA samples in the field requires careful planning, attention to detail, and adherence to ethical and legal considerations. Here are some procedures for collecting DNA samples in the field:

- Select Suitable Samples: Identify potential sources of DNA, such as hair, scat (feces), saliva, blood, or tissue. Focus on non-invasive sampling methods to minimize harm to the animals.
- Use Sterile Equipment: Use clean, disposable gloves and sterile sampling tools to prevent contamination of the DNA samples.
- Minimize Handling: Minimize direct contact with the samples to avoid transferring human DNA onto the collected material.
- Hair Samples: When collecting hair samples, use clean forceps or tweezers to gently pluck a few hairs from areas where they are loosely attached to the animal's body, such as shedding or caught on branches.
- Scat Samples: Use a clean spatula or scoop to collect a small portion of the scat. Avoid touching the sample with your hands.

- Saliva or Blood Samples: If collecting saliva or blood, use swabs or a sterile needle and syringe to obtain the sample from wounds or areas where the animal has recently left saliva.
- Tissue Samples: Collecting tissue samples requires specific training and permits in many jurisdictions. It is best to leave tissue collection to professionals with the necessary expertise.
- Labeling and Documentation: Properly label each sample with information such as the date, time, location, species (if known), and any relevant observations. Keep detailed field notes for each sample collected.
- Preservation: Store the samples in appropriate containers and preservatives to maintain DNA integrity. Commonly used preservatives include silica gel, ethanol, or specialized DNA preservation solutions.
- Chain of Custody: If the samples are for scientific research or legal purposes, establish and maintain a proper chain of custody to ensure the integrity of the evidence.
- Permits and Regulations: Familiarize yourself with local regulations and obtain any necessary permits for collecting DNA samples from wildlife.
- Ethical Considerations: Collect DNA samples with respect for the animals and their habitats. Minimize disturbance and harm to the species and ecosystem.
- Collaborate with Experts: If you are unsure about proper DNA sampling techniques or require specialized analysis, collaborate with experts in the field of genetics and DNA research.
- Data Sharing: Consider sharing your DNA samples and data with reputable research institutions or experts to contribute to a broader understanding of wildlife genetics.

Remember that collecting DNA samples from wildlife requires special attention and prudence. Consult subject-matter experts or relevant wildlife authorities if you are uncertain about appropriate procedures or concerned about the outcomes of your sample.

Environmental DNA sampling

By gathering and examining DNA that organisms shed or release into the environment, environmental DNA (eDNA) sampling is a non-invasive technique for finding and studying the presence of organisms in their natural habitats. Because the eDNA approach can identify species without requiring physical capture or direct observation, it has become more popular in the fields of ecology, conservation biology, and environmental monitoring.

Here's how eDNA sampling works:

- DNA Shedding: All living organisms continuously shed DNA into their environment through various biological materials, such as skin cells, feces, urine, mucus, and hair.
- Sample Collection: Environmental DNA sampling involves collecting water, soil, sediment, or air samples from the environment where the target species might be present.
- Filtering and Extraction: In aquatic environments, water samples are typically filtered to capture the eDNA, while in terrestrial environments, soil and sediment samples are processed to extract the eDNA.
- PCR Amplification: Polymerase chain reaction (PCR) is then used to amplify and replicate the target species' DNA fragments, making them detectable.
- Species Identification: Once amplified, the DNA is sequenced and compared to existing DNA databases to identify the species present in the sample.

Environmental DNA sampling offers several advantages:

- Non-invasive: It does not require direct contact with the target species, reducing disturbance and potential harm to the animals.
- Sensitive: eDNA sampling can detect even rare or elusive species that might be challenging to observe directly.
- Efficient: It allows researchers to survey large areas quickly, increasing the efficiency of species detection.
- Early Detection: It can be used for early detection of invasive species or endangered species monitoring.
- Biodiversity Assessment: It provides valuable information on species presence and distribution, contributing to biodiversity assessments.

However, eDNA sampling also has some limitations:

- Detection Limit: The technique might not detect species that are present in low abundance or have limited shedding rates.
- Degradation: Environmental DNA can degrade over time, limiting the detection window for some species.
- Contamination: Contamination from other sources can lead to false positives or inaccurate results.
- Lack of Species-Specificity: The eDNA collected might belong to closely related species, requiring further analysis for accurate identification.

Despite these drawbacks, eDNA sampling is a useful tool for ecological and conservation study, and it is constantly developing thanks to new techniques and technologies. It advances our knowledge of species distribution and ecosystem dynamics and serves as a supplement to conventional field survey techniques.

Chapter 31

Using Social Media

Social media can be a powerful tool for collecting sighting reports of Bigfoot or any other cryptid or elusive creature. Here are some ways social media can assist in gathering such reports:

Dedicated Social Media Pages:

- Create dedicated social media pages or groups focused on Bigfoot sightings and research. Encourage users to share their experiences, photos, and videos related to Bigfoot sightings.

Hashtags:

- Use specific hashtags like #BigfootSighting, #Cryptozoology, or #BigfootEncounter to make it easier for people to find and share their sightings. Encourage others to use these hashtags when posting about Bigfoot encounters.

Engaging Content:

- Post engaging and informative content related to Bigfoot, such as videos, articles, and photos. This can attract more people interested in the subject and prompt them to share their own experiences.

Online Surveys:

- Create online surveys or questionnaires using platforms like Google Forms or SurveyMonkey to gather structured information about Bigfoot sightings. Share these surveys on social media and encourage people to participate.

Location Tagging:

- Ask people to share their sightings along with the location details. This can help you map the sightings and identify potential hotspots for further investigation.

Live Q&A Sessions:

- Host live Q&A sessions on social media platforms where people can ask questions or share their experiences directly with you. This interactive approach can lead to more engagement and real-time responses.

Partnerships:

- Collaborate with other Bigfoot researchers or enthusiasts on social media to increase your reach and engagement. Cross-promote each other's content to reach a wider audience.

Social Media Advertising:

- Consider using social media advertising to reach a broader audience and encourage people to report their Bigfoot sightings.

Visual Content:

- Encourage people to share photos or videos if they have captured any potential evidence of Bigfoot sightings. Visual evidence can generate more interest and credibility.

Respect and Validation:

- Show respect to those who share their encounters and validate their experiences. This will encourage more people to come forward with their stories.

Data Collection Platform:

- Develop a website or platform where people can submit their Bigfoot sightings in a structured manner. Share the link on social media to direct users to the reporting platform.

Adhere to scientific rigour when assessing the information gathered. Real reports, hoaxes, and misidentifications are likely to be mixed in with the data, therefore it's critical to thoroughly filter through it to separate fact from fiction.

Chapter 32

Using YouTube

Using YouTube to collect sighting reports of Bigfoot can be an effective and engaging way to gather information from the public. Here's a step-by-step guide on how you can use YouTube for this purpose:

Create a YouTube Channel:

- If you don't already have one, create a YouTube channel dedicated to Bigfoot sightings and research. Choose a channel name that is relevant and easy to remember.

Set the Tone and Purpose:

- Clearly communicate the purpose of your channel in the channel description. Let viewers know that you are interested in collecting credible sighting reports and evidence related to Bigfoot.

Upload Informational Videos:

- Start by uploading informational videos about Bigfoot, including its history, reported sightings, and other relevant details. This will attract people interested in the topic to your channel.

Encourage Submissions:

- In your videos and channel description, encourage viewers to share their Bigfoot sighting reports and evidence with you. Ask them to submit their stories, photos, videos, or any other relevant information.

Create a Submission Guidelines Video:

- Make a dedicated video explaining the guidelines for submitting sighting reports. Clearly outline the information you need, such as date, location, description of the sighting, and any supporting evidence.

Engage with Your Audience:

- Respond to comments and messages from viewers. Engage with your audience to build a sense of community and trust.

Share Contact Information:

- Provide an email address or other contact details in your video descriptions and channel about section, where viewers can send their sighting reports privately.

Curate and Review Submissions:

- Regularly review and verify the sighting reports and evidence you receive. Exercise caution to ensure you only share credible and genuine information with your audience.

Create Compilation Videos:

- Compile credible sighting reports into videos, crediting the individuals who provided the information (if they consent to being credited). This can help showcase the diversity and volume of sightings reported to your channel.

Respect Privacy and Consent:

- Always respect the privacy of those who submit reports and obtain their permission before using their content in your videos.

Promote Your Channel:

- Share your videos on social media platforms and Bigfoot-related forums to reach a wider audience and encourage more submissions.

Remain Objective:

- While collecting sightings, maintain an objective and scientific approach. Avoid sensationalizing or promoting unfounded claims.

Remember that while compiling Bigfoot encounter stories from YouTube may be an interesting project, honesty and authenticity must be upheld at all times. Submissions must be rigorously assessed, and one should approach them with suspicion because some of them might be fakes or misidentifications.

Chapter 33

Google Maps and Google Earth

Technological developments have completely changed the data collection and analysis methods used by wildlife researchers in recent years. Google Maps is one of these developments that has proven to be quite helpful for wildlife researchers who are trying to learn about and protect the natural environment. This chapter examines the different ways that Google Maps can be used as a resource for wildlife research, emphasizing the advantages and future uses of this tool.

Habitat Mapping

Identifying and charting animal habitats is one of the core components of wildlife study. Researchers can examine landscapes, vegetation types, and geographical characteristics that affect species distributions using Google Maps' satellite imagery and street view features. These variables can be investigated by scientists to produce thorough habitat maps that help with species behaviour research and conservation efforts.

Migration Patterns

Google Maps' global reach and continuous satellite coverage make it an ideal resource for studying wildlife migration patterns. Researchers can track the movements of migratory species, such as birds, marine animals, and large mammals, by analyzing historical satellite data. Understanding migration routes and timing is crucial for implementing measures to protect these species during their arduous journeys.

Biodiversity Monitoring

Biodiversity monitoring is essential for assessing ecosystem health and identifying areas of conservation concern. Google Maps, in combination with citizen science initiatives, allows researchers to crowdsource biodiversity data. Researchers can invite the public to report wildlife sightings, helping build a comprehensive database of species distribution and abundance. This approach fosters community engagement and empowers citizens to actively participate in wildlife conservation.

Human-Wildlife Conflict Analysis

As human populations expand, conflicts with wildlife become more common. Google Maps aids researchers in analyzing areas with high instances of human-wildlife conflicts. By examining patterns of animal encounters and human activities, researchers can propose and implement strategies to mitigate conflicts, such as designing wildlife corridors or improving agricultural practices.

Estimating Population Densities

When used in conjunction with cutting-edge remote sensing methods, Google Maps enables researchers to calculate wildlife population densities. Researchers can discover animal counts and create statistical models to predict population sizes within particular regions by examining satellite photos. Planning for conservation efforts and tracking population patterns over time both greatly benefit from this knowledge.

Assessing Habitat Fragmentation

Habitat fragmentation is a significant threat to wildlife populations worldwide. Google Maps can provide detailed information on land-use changes and habitat fragmentation, enabling researchers to pinpoint areas that require urgent conservation attention. Analyzing historical satellite imagery allows scientists to track changes in landscapes and evaluate the impact on wildlife populations.

Monitoring Environmental Changes

Wildlife habitats are strongly impacted by climate change and other environmental factors. Researchers are able to visually evaluate changes in landscapes over extensive time periods by utilizing Google Maps' historical satellite images and the street view time-lapse capability. This information contributes to our understanding of how species distribution, behaviour, and overall ecosystem dynamics are impacted by climate change.

Conclusion

By giving researchers an effective and user-friendly tool for understanding and protecting the natural world, Google Maps has changed the field of wildlife study. It provides unmatched opportunities for mapping habitats, evaluating migration patterns, monitoring biodiversity, and much more thanks to its satellite imaging, street view, and historical data. Google Maps' connection with other cutting-edge tools will certainly result in additional developments in wildlife research as technology develops, ultimately contributing to the preservation of Earth's priceless biodiversity.

Chapter 34

Bigfoot Hoaxers and Pranksters

Those who falsely claim to have seen Bigfoot or to have seen it in order to trick, amuse, or control others. By spreading misleading information and making dramatic claims, they add to the frequently complicated field of Bigfoot study, making it more challenging for serious researchers to distinguish between reality and fiction. Pranksters and hoaxers can use a range of techniques to carry out their plots, from complex setups to more basic misrepresentations.

Motivations: Why Hoax?

There are many different reasons why people pull practical jokes and hoaxes, such as entertainment, fame-seeking, attention-seeking, or even money. While some people could take pleasure in tricking others, others might utilize hoaxes as satire or societal criticism. HOAXES can take advantage of people's natural interest, fascination, and openness to believing in the paranormal in the context of Bigfoot study..

Methods: How Hoaxes are Created

Hoaxers often use a combination of physical evidence, staged photographs, and fabricated eyewitness accounts to create a convincing narrative. They may plant fake footprints, construct artificial nests or shelters, and even produce counterfeit audio recordings purportedly capturing Bigfoot vocalizations. In some cases, they may manipulate existing evidence, such as altering or doctoring photographs to make them appear more convincing.

Famous Hoaxes and Pranks

People pull practical jokes and hoaxes for a variety of purposes, including amusement, attention-seeking, celebrity, or even financial gain. Some may find amusement in deceiving others, but others may use hoaxes as satire or a critique of society. In the context of Bigfoot research, HOAXES can profit from people's innate curiosity, fascination, and openness to believing in the paranormal.

Impact on Research and Belief

Research on Bigfoot and public opinion have been greatly impacted by the existence of hoaxers and pranksters. Sincere researchers frequently find it difficult to distinguish between well-constructed hoaxes and real evidence. This relationship breeds doubt and occasionally damages the reputation of Bigfoot research as a whole. Furthermore, the prevalence of hoaxes might make it difficult for people to distinguish between credible and unreliable sources of information, which could have an impact on the likelihood that real discoveries will be given due consideration.

Unmasking Hoaxes: The Role of Critical Analysis

Critical analysis has been increasingly useful in identifying hoaxes as Bigfoot study advances. Researchers and aficionados are getting better at examining evidence closely to look for photographic manipulations, inconsistencies, and differences in the accounts of eyewitnesses. Working together and having candid conversations within the scientific community can help reveal frauds and make the process of researching the phenomenon more transparent and reliable.

The existence of hoaxers and pranksters in the field of Bigfoot study highlights the importance of strict scientific technique, critical thinking, and a dedication to distinguishing fact from fiction. While hoaxes have the potential to undermine the search for the truth, they can serve as a helpful reminder of the difficulties and complexities involved in looking into mysterious events.

Chapter 35

Top Ten Scientists Conducting Bigfoot Research

These individuals have applied scientific methods and expertise to investigate the mysteries surrounding the elusive creature known as Bigfoot.

- Dr. Jeff Meldrum: A renowned professor of anatomy and anthropology at Idaho State University, Dr. Meldrum is considered a leading authority on Bigfoot research. He has extensively studied alleged Bigfoot footprints and advocated for the scientific investigation of the phenomenon.
- Dr. Jane Goodall: While primarily known for her groundbreaking work with chimpanzees, Dr. Goodall has expressed an open-minded perspective on the existence of undiscovered large primates, such as Bigfoot, and has supported further research.
- Dr. Todd Disotell: An evolutionary anthropologist and a molecular primatologist at New York University, Dr. Disotell has analyzed DNA samples from purported Bigfoot evidence to determine their origins.
- Dr. John Bindernagel: A wildlife biologist and author, Dr. Bindernagel has researched Bigfoot sightings and vocalizations, advocating for a scientific approach to studying these reports. (1941–2018)

- Dr. Brian Sykes: A geneticist at the University of Oxford, Dr. Sykes conducted a study examining hair samples attributed to Bigfoot, though the results were inconclusive.
- Dr. Anna Nekaris: A primatologist at Oxford Brookes University, Dr. Nekaris has expressed interest in cryptozoology and has discussed the possibility of undiscovered primates like Bigfoot.
- Dr. Bryan Sykes: Another geneticist and author, Dr. Sykes has also investigated potential Bigfoot DNA evidence and published his findings in his book "Bigfoot, Yeti, and the Last Neanderthal."
- Dr. Russell Mittermeier: A primatologist and president of Conservation International, Dr. Mittermeier has acknowledged the potential existence of unknown large primates in remote regions.
- Dr. George Schaller: A field biologist and conservationist, Dr. Schaller's work with endangered species has led him to acknowledge the possibility of unknown primate species, including Bigfoot.
- Dr. Loren Coleman: A cryptozoologist and author, Dr. Coleman has been a prominent figure in the study of cryptids, including Bigfoot, and has contributed to the dissemination of information about the subject.

These scholars have demonstrated a desire to learn more about the subject and a readiness to look at published data. Their contributions have improved the body of knowledge about Bigfoot research and created avenues for more in-depth analysis of this fascinating phenomenon.

Chapter 36

Top Ten Bigfoot Researchers

Top ten prominent Bigfoot researchers who have dedicated their time and efforts to the investigation of the elusive creature known as Bigfoot.

- Bob Gimlin: As one of the witnesses of the famous Patterson-Gimlin film, Bob Gimlin has been an influential figure in the Bigfoot research community. He has shared his experiences and insights from the famous encounter.
- Cliff Barackman: Known for his appearances on the TV show "Finding Bigfoot," Cliff Barackman is a Bigfoot field researcher and evidence analyst who has conducted numerous investigations across North America.
- Kathy Strain: An active field researcher and author, Kathy Strain has contributed valuable research to the study of Bigfoot, with a particular focus on eyewitness testimonies and historical accounts.
- Dr. Jeff Meldrum: Mentioned previously in this handbook, Dr. Meldrum's expertise in anatomy and anthropology has led him to thoroughly investigate the footprints and possible existence of Bigfoot.
- Thomas Steenburg: A veteran Bigfoot researcher with decades of experience, Thomas Steenburg has conducted extensive field investigations and written books on the subject.

- Autumn Williams: As part of the "Finding Bigfoot" team, Autumn Williams has been involved in numerous expeditions and field investigations, adding to her expertise as a Bigfoot researcher.
- Paul Freeman: Known for his controversial video footage and footprint discoveries, the late Paul Freeman dedicated much of his life to Bigfoot research.
- Dr. John Bindernagel: Also mentioned previously, Dr. Bindernagel's background in wildlife biology has led him to explore Bigfoot sightings and vocalizations with a scientific approach.
- René Dahinden: A pioneer in Bigfoot research, René Dahinden's field investigations and contributions to the subject have left a lasting impact on the Bigfoot community.
- Loren Coleman: An accomplished cryptozoologist and author, Loren Coleman has extensively written about various cryptids, including Bigfoot, and has been a prominent figure in the field.

The aforementioned ten researchers have achieved noteworthy advancements in the field of Bigfoot study via their diligent work, written works, and investigations. Their combined efforts have increased awareness and interest in this elusive species while also helping to unravel some of the mysteries surrounding Bigfoot.

Chapter 37

Top 10 Bigfoot Research Groups

List of the top 10 well-known Bigfoot research teams that have teamed together to look into the mysterious Bigfoot species. These organizations are committed to using scientific techniques, carrying out fieldwork, and educating the public about Bigfoot.

- **Bigfoot Field Researchers Organization (BFRO):** One of the largest and most well-known Bigfoot research groups, the BFRO has a vast database of reported sightings, tracks, and encounters. They conduct field expeditions and investigations across North America.
- **North American Wood Ape Conservancy (NAWAC):** Focused on researching the elusive "wood ape" or Bigfoot in the southern United States, NAWAC conducts extensive field investigations and promotes scientific inquiry.
- **Gulf Coast Bigfoot Research Organization (GCBRO):** Dedicated to investigating Bigfoot sightings and encounters in the Gulf Coast region of the United States, the GCBRO actively engages in field research and documentary efforts.
- **Sasquatch Genome Project:** Founded by Dr. Melba Ketchum, the Sasquatch Genome Project aims to analyze purported Bigfoot DNA evidence to understand the creature's genetic makeup.

- **Bigfoot Investigations of the Rockies (BIRO):** Concentrating on the Rocky Mountains region, BIRO conducts field expeditions and collects data related to Bigfoot sightings and activity.
- **Pennsylvania Bigfoot Society (PBS):** Focusing on Bigfoot research in Pennsylvania and surrounding states, PBS collaborates with witnesses and fellow researchers to investigate reported encounters.
- **British Columbia Scientific Cryptozoology Club (BCSCC):** Operating in British Columbia, Canada, BCSCC investigates various cryptids, including Bigfoot, with a scientific approach.
- **Southeastern Ohio Society for Bigfoot Investigation (SOSBI):** Focused on investigating Bigfoot sightings and encounters in southeastern Ohio, SOSBI conducts field expeditions and educates the public about Bigfoot.
- **Australian Yowie Research:** This group is dedicated to researching the Yowie, Australia's version of Bigfoot, and investigates reported sightings and encounters in the region.
- **Olympic Project:** Focused on the Olympic Peninsula in Washington State, this group conducts field research and collects evidence related to Bigfoot sightings in the region. These Bigfoot research organizations have significantly advanced the field through their fieldwork, data gathering, and public education efforts.

Chapter 38

Famous Quotes and Reflections on Bigfoot

Let's examine some well-known assertions and analyses of the enigmatic Bigfoot made by experts, enthusiasts, and well-known people. These sayings capture the allure and mystique of Bigfoot just right.

- "The fact that the legend of Bigfoot has persisted for centuries across diverse cultures is a testament to the enduring allure of the unknown." - Anonymous
- "Bigfoot represents the wildness that still exists in the world, reminding us that there are mysteries left to explore." - Jane Goodall, Primatologist
- "Whether Bigfoot is a flesh-and-blood creature or a myth, its legend has become a part of our cultural tapestry, speaking to our innate curiosity about the unknown." - Loren Coleman, Cryptozoologist
- "The mystery of Bigfoot serves as a reminder that even in the age of satellites and smartphones, there are still secrets waiting to be unraveled in the vast wilderness." - Jeff Meldrum, Anthropologist
- "As a researcher, I may not have definitive proof of Bigfoot's existence, but the journey of exploration and discovery has enriched my life beyond measure." - John Bindernagel, Wildlife Biologist
- "The quest for Bigfoot is not merely about finding a creature; it's about finding ourselves in the vastness of nature and embracing the wonder of the unknown." - Mary Grefe, Naturalist
- "In Indigenous cultures, the legend of Bigfoot is woven into their traditions, preserving the wisdom of their ancestors and the reverence for the natural world." - Chief Dan George, Indigenous Elder
- "Bigfoot may be an elusive creature, but its legend has fostered a sense of unity among researchers and enthusiasts from all walks of life." - Bobo Fay, Bigfoot Enthusiast
- "In the search for Bigfoot, we find camaraderie, adventure, and a shared passion for exploring the mysteries that lie beyond the limits of our understanding." - Cliff Barackman, Bigfoot Field Researcher
- "The legacy of Bigfoot research extends beyond the quest for evidence. It has sparked a curiosity that drives us to continuously explore and appreciate the wonders of the natural world." - Josh Gates, Explorer and TV Host
- "While the evidence for Bigfoot remains inconclusive, the pursuit of this legendary creature encourages us to question, to explore, and to never lose our sense of wonder." - Anonymous

- "It's not the destination that's important, when it comes to researching Bigfoot, it's the journey" Timothy D, Field Researcher, Author

I hope these statements encourage you to keep exploring and learning, whether it's in the hunt for Bigfoot or solving the many other mysteries that lie in wait in the unexplored parts of our planet.

Chapter 38

State and Provincial Bigfoot Hotspots:

British Columbia, Canada

British Columbia is a vast and diverse province with a rich history of Bigfoot sightings and encounters, making it a popular destination for Bigfoot researchers and enthusiasts.

The Pacific Northwest and British Columbia

The Pacific Northwest, including parts of British Columbia, has a long history of Bigfoot sightings and legends. The dense forests, rugged mountains, and vast wilderness areas in this region provide ideal habitats for an elusive creature like Bigfoot.

Harrison Hot Springs

Located in the Fraser Valley, Harrison Hot Springs is known for its natural hot springs and scenic beauty. It has also gained a reputation as a Bigfoot hotspot due to numerous reported sightings and encounters in the surrounding wilderness.

Sasquatch Provincial Park

As the name suggests, Sasquatch Provincial Park, located near Harrison Hot Springs, is a designated area with a history of Bigfoot sightings. The park offers beautiful trails and camping opportunities, attracting both nature enthusiasts and Bigfoot researchers.

Chehalis Lake

Chehalis Lake, located in the Fraser Valley, is another Bigfoot hotspot. The remote location and dense forest surrounding the lake have led to various reported encounters and intriguing evidence over the years.

Bella Coola

Bella Coola, situated in the Central Coast region of British Columbia, is known for its stunning landscapes and diverse wildlife. It is also an area with a history of Bigfoot sightings, adding to the allure of this picturesque location for Bigfoot researchers.

Harrison Lake

Harrison Lake is another hotbed of Bigfoot activity in British Columbia. The lake's secluded shoreline and proximity to wilderness areas make it an appealing spot for researchers hoping to catch a glimpse of the elusive creature.

Tantalus Range

The Tantalus Range, part of the Coast Mountains in British Columbia, is known for its rugged terrain and pristine wilderness. It has also been associated with Bigfoot sightings and encounters, drawing researchers to explore its remote and mysterious landscapes.

Vancouver Island

Vancouver Island, located off the southwestern coast of British Columbia, has a long history of Bigfoot sightings. The island's vast forests and rugged mountains provide potential habitats for the elusive creature.

Nahmint Valley

Nahmint Valley, situated on Vancouver Island, is another area that has gained attention from Bigfoot researchers. The valley's remote location and reported sightings make it an intriguing destination for those hoping to study Bigfoot in its natural habitat.

Northern British Columbia

The northern regions of British Columbia, with their vast wilderness and remote areas, are also considered potential Bigfoot hotspots. These less-explored regions offer ample opportunities for researchers to investigate reported sightings and conduct fieldwork.

Washington State USA

Washington State is renowned for its dense forests, rugged mountains, and vast wilderness, making it a prime location for reported Bigfoot sightings and encounters.

The Pacific Northwest

The Pacific Northwest, which includes Washington State, is considered a hotspot for Bigfoot activity. The region's lush forests, abundant wildlife, and remote areas create an ideal habitat for an elusive creature like Bigfoot.

Mount St. Helens

Mount St. Helens, famous for its volcanic eruption in 1980, is also associated with Bigfoot sightings. The surrounding wilderness and remote areas around the mountain have attracted researchers and enthusiasts looking for evidence of Bigfoot's presence.

Gifford Pinchot National Forest

Gifford Pinchot National Forest, located in southern Washington, is a vast and diverse area known for its recreational opportunities and natural beauty. It is also recognized as a Bigfoot hotspot, with reported encounters and evidence gathered by researchers over the years.

Olympic National Forest

Olympic National Forest, situated on the Olympic Peninsula, is another area in Washington with a history of reported Bigfoot sightings. The forest's dense canopy and rugged terrain make it an intriguing location for Bigfoot research.

Ape Canyon

Ape Canyon, near Mount St. Helens, is famous for a historic encounter with alleged Bigfoot creatures in the early 1920s. The incident involved a group of miners who claimed to have encountered aggressive ape-like creatures in the canyon, leading to its name.

Mount Adams

Mount Adams, part of the Cascade Range, is known for both its natural beauty and Bigfoot activity. Researchers and enthusiasts have reported sightings and unexplained phenomena in the vicinity of this majestic peak.

Yakima Valley

Yakima Valley, located in south-central Washington, has also gained attention for reported Bigfoot sightings. The valley's mix of farmland, forests, and remote areas makes it an interesting location for potential Bigfoot encounters.

Colville National Forest

Colville National Forest, in northeastern Washington, is a vast and diverse forested area known for its wildlife and recreational opportunities. It has also been associated with Bigfoot sightings and activity.

Wenatchee National Forest

Wenatchee National Forest, located in central Washington, is another region where Bigfoot sightings have been reported. Its expansive wilderness and mountainous terrain offer potential habitats for the elusive creature.

Gifford Pinchot National Forest

Gifford Pinchot National Forest, situated in southwestern Washington, is not only a popular outdoor destination but also a place where Bigfoot sightings and encounters have been documented.

Idaho, USA

Idaho's vast and diverse wilderness areas, including dense forests, rugged mountains, and remote backcountry, have made it a region of interest for Bigfoot enthusiasts and researchers.

The Wilderness of Idaho

Idaho is known for its rugged and untouched wilderness, providing ample opportunities for potential Bigfoot encounters. Let's explore some of the notable hotspots:

Payette National Forest

Payette National Forest, located in central Idaho, is a vast expanse of forested lands and rugged mountains. It has a history of reported Bigfoot sightings, making it an intriguing area for researchers and enthusiasts.

Sawtooth National Recreation Area

Sawtooth National Recreation Area, nestled in the Sawtooth Mountains of central Idaho, is another location where Bigfoot activity has been reported. The area's scenic beauty and remote backcountry make it an attractive destination for researchers.

Clearwater National Forest

Clearwater National Forest, situated in north-central Idaho, is known for its dense forests and abundant wildlife. The forest has been associated with Bigfoot sightings and encounters over the years.

Selway-Bitterroot Wilderness

The Selway-Bitterroot Wilderness, spanning Idaho and Montana, offers a vast and rugged wilderness that has gained attention for alleged Bigfoot activity. Its remote and pristine landscapes make it a prime location for potential Bigfoot encounters.

Pocatello Mountains

The Pocatello Mountains in southeastern Idaho have also been mentioned in connection with Bigfoot sightings. The region's remote and rugged terrain adds to its appeal for Bigfoot researchers.

Panhandle National Forest

Panhandle National Forest, located in the northern part of Idaho, has a mix of dense forests and mountainous terrain. It has been the site of reported Bigfoot encounters, attracting researchers to explore its wilderness.

Frank Church-River of No Return Wilderness

The Frank Church-River of No Return Wilderness, one of the largest wilderness areas in the contiguous United States, is located in central Idaho. This vast and rugged region has also been associated with Bigfoot sightings.

Lochsa River Area

The Lochsa River area in northern Idaho is known for its pristine wilderness and dense forests. It has been mentioned in reports of Bigfoot sightings and potential activity.

Coeur d'Alene National Forest

Coeur d'Alene National Forest, situated in northern Idaho, offers a diverse landscape of forests and lakes. It has been a location of interest for Bigfoot researchers investigating reported encounters in the region.

California, USA

California, with its diverse landscapes ranging from dense forests to rugged mountains and remote wilderness areas, has a long history of reported Bigfoot sightings and encounters.

The Golden State and Bigfoot

California's vast and varied terrain provides potential habitats for Bigfoot, making it an area of interest for researchers and enthusiasts alike.

Bluff Creek - Six Rivers National Forest

Bluff Creek, located in the Six Rivers National Forest in northern California, is famous for the iconic Patterson-Gimlin film, which captured a purported Bigfoot creature in 1967. The area around Bluff Creek continues to be a hotbed of Bigfoot research and activity.

Sierra Nevada Mountains

The Sierra Nevada Mountains, stretching across eastern California, have a long history of Bigfoot sightings. The region's remote and rugged landscapes, including the infamous "Sierra Kills" incident, have added to its reputation as a Bigfoot hotspot.

Redwood National and State Parks

Redwood National and State Parks, situated along the northern California coast, are known for their ancient redwood forests and diverse wildlife. This region has also been associated with Bigfoot encounters over the years.

Marble Mountain Wilderness

Marble Mountain Wilderness, located in the Klamath Mountains of northern California, is another area with reported Bigfoot activity. The wilderness's rugged and dense terrain provides potential hiding places for an elusive creature.

San Bernardino National Forest

San Bernardino National Forest, in southern California, has a mix of forested areas and mountains. It has been mentioned in reports of Bigfoot sightings, drawing interest from researchers.

Shasta-Trinity National Forest

Shasta-Trinity National Forest, covering a vast area in northern California, has also been the site of reported Bigfoot encounters. The forest's diverse landscapes make it an attractive location for investigations.

Inyo National Forest

Inyo National Forest, located in the eastern Sierra Nevada region of California, is another area that has gained attention for alleged Bigfoot activity. Its remote and mountainous terrain adds to its allure for researchers.

Santa Cruz Mountains

The Santa Cruz Mountains, situated in the San Francisco Bay Area, have a history of reported Bigfoot sightings. The proximity to populated areas has led to numerous eyewitness accounts in this region.

Yosemite National Park

Yosemite National Park, one of California's most iconic parks, has also been mentioned in reports of Bigfoot encounters. The park's vast wilderness and dense forests provide potential habitats for the elusive creature.

Alaska, USA

Alaska, the largest and most remote state in the United States. Alaska's vast wilderness, rugged terrain, and sparse population have made it an intriguing location for reported Bigfoot sightings and encounters.

The Wilds of Alaska

Alaska's vast and untamed wilderness offers plenty of potential habitats for an elusive creature like Bigfoot, making it an area of interest for researchers and adventurers.

Tongass National Forest

Tongass National Forest, the largest national forest in the United States, is located in southeastern Alaska. This vast expanse of forested land has been associated with Bigfoot sightings and activity.

Chugach National Forest

Chugach National Forest, located in south-central Alaska, is another area where Bigfoot encounters have been reported. Its remote and diverse landscapes attract outdoor enthusiasts and researchers alike.

Denali National Park and Preserve

Denali National Park, home to the tallest peak in North America, has also gained attention for alleged Bigfoot sightings. The park's expansive wilderness and rugged terrain provide potential hiding places for the creature.

Kodiak Island

Kodiak Island, located in the Gulf of Alaska, is known for its rugged and isolated landscapes. The island has also been mentioned in connection with Bigfoot sightings and encounters.

Alaska Triangle

The Alaska Triangle, an area stretching from Juneau to Anchorage and Barrow, has been associated with mysterious disappearances and strange phenomena, including reported Bigfoot sightings.

Hatcher Pass

Hatcher Pass, situated in the Talkeetna Mountains of south-central Alaska, is another location that has gained attention from Bigfoot researchers.

Wrangell-St. Elias National Park and Preserve

Wrangell-St. Elias National Park, the largest national park in the United States, offers expansive wilderness and diverse landscapes. This remote region has also been mentioned in reports of Bigfoot encounters.

Kenai Peninsula

The Kenai Peninsula, known for its stunning landscapes and abundant wildlife, has also been associated with Bigfoot sightings and activity.

Arctic Regions

Even in Alaska's remote Arctic regions, there have been reports of Bigfoot-like creatures. These remote and icy landscapes add to the mystery of Bigfoot sightings in the state.

Yukon, Canada

The Yukon's vast and remote wilderness, characterized by dense forests, rugged mountains, and expansive tundra, has made it an area of interest for reported Bigfoot sightings and encounters.

The Wilds of the Yukon

The Yukon's vast and untamed landscapes offer plenty of potential habitats for an elusive creature like Bigfoot, attracting researchers and enthusiasts to explore its mysteries.

Kluane National Park and Reserve

Kluane National Park, located in southwestern Yukon, is known for its towering mountains and glaciers. This remote and pristine wilderness has been associated with Bigfoot sightings and activity.

Whitehorse Area

The region around Whitehorse, Yukon's capital city, has also been mentioned in connection with Bigfoot encounters. The city's proximity to wilderness areas makes it an interesting location for potential research.

Tombstone Territorial Park

Tombstone Territorial Park, situated in central Yukon, offers striking landscapes and diverse wildlife. This region has also been associated with Bigfoot sightings and reported encounters.

Dempster Highway

The Dempster Highway, stretching from Yukon to the Northwest Territories, is a remote and scenic route. It has been mentioned in reports of Bigfoot-like creatures sighted along the highway.

Teslin Lake

Teslin Lake, located in southern Yukon, is known for its wilderness and recreational opportunities. This area has also been mentioned in connection with Bigfoot encounters.

Stewart River

The Stewart River, winding through central Yukon, is another region where Bigfoot activity has been reported. Its remote and pristine environment adds to the allure for potential research.

Northern Tutchone Region

The Northern Tutchone region, inhabited by the First Nations people of Yukon, has a rich cultural history with stories of encounters with mysterious creatures, including Bigfoot-like beings.

Watson Lake

Watson Lake, in southeastern Yukon, has also been associated with Bigfoot sightings. The area's wilderness and proximity to British Columbia make it an interesting location for potential research.

Klondike Region

The Klondike region, famous for the gold rush history, has also been mentioned in reports of Bigfoot sightings. Its rugged landscapes and remote nature offer potential habitats for an elusive creature.

Alberta, Canada

Welcome to Chapter 24 of "The Bigfoot Hunters Handbook." In this chapter, we will explore some of the well-known Bigfoot hotspots in Alberta, Canada. Alberta's diverse landscapes, which include mountains, forests, and vast wilderness areas, have made it an area of interest for reported Bigfoot sightings and encounters.

The Wilderness of Alberta

Alberta's wilderness offers a wide range of potential habitats for Bigfoot, attracting researchers and enthusiasts to explore the possibility of this elusive creature's presence.

Canadian Rockies

The Canadian Rockies, stretching through western Alberta, are famous for their stunning beauty and rugged terrain. This mountainous region has been associated with reported Bigfoot sightings.

Jasper National Park

Jasper National Park, located in the Canadian Rockies, is known for its pristine wilderness and abundant wildlife. It has also gained attention for alleged Bigfoot activity.

Banff National Park

Banff National Park, another iconic destination in the Canadian Rockies, has been mentioned in reports of Bigfoot encounters. The park's vast and remote backcountry provides potential hiding places for the elusive creature.

Kananaskis Country

Kananaskis Country, situated west of Calgary, is known for its recreational opportunities and natural beauty. This region has also been associated with Bigfoot sightings.

Nordegg Area

The Nordegg area, located in the foothills of the Canadian Rockies, has been mentioned in connection with Bigfoot encounters.

Athabasca River

The Athabasca River, flowing through central Alberta, has also been associated with reported Bigfoot sightings in its wilderness surroundings.

Bighorn Country

Bighorn Country, located in west-central Alberta, is known for its rugged landscapes and diverse wildlife. This area has also been mentioned in reports of Bigfoot activity.

Willmore Wilderness Park

Willmore Wilderness Park, situated in west-central Alberta, offers remote and pristine backcountry that has been associated with alleged Bigfoot sightings.

Ghost Wilderness Area

The Ghost Wilderness Area, located west of Calgary, has been mentioned in connection with Bigfoot encounters.

Oregon, USA

Oregon's diverse landscapes, which include dense forests, rugged mountains, and vast wilderness areas, have made it a popular location for reported Bigfoot sightings and encounters.

The Pacific Northwest and Bigfoot

Oregon is part of the Pacific Northwest, an area with a long history of Bigfoot sightings and legends. The region's lush forests, rugged terrain, and remote locations create an ideal habitat for an elusive creature like Bigfoot.

Mount Hood National Forest

Mount Hood National Forest, located in north-central Oregon, is known for its iconic mountain and dense forests. This region has been associated with reported Bigfoot sightings.

Deschutes National Forest

Deschutes National Forest, situated in central Oregon, is another area where Bigfoot encounters have been reported. The forest's diverse landscapes attract outdoor enthusiasts and researchers.

Willamette National Forest

Willamette National Forest, located in western Oregon, is known for its abundant wildlife and natural beauty. This region has also been associated with alleged Bigfoot activity.

Clackamas County

Clackamas County, south of Portland, Oregon, has gained attention for reported Bigfoot sightings in its wooded areas.

Mount Jefferson Wilderness

Mount Jefferson Wilderness, in the central part of the state, is another location that has been mentioned in connection with Bigfoot encounters.

Siskiyou Mountains

The Siskiyou Mountains, located in southwestern Oregon, have a history of Bigfoot sightings and activity.

Umpqua National Forest

Umpqua National Forest, situated in southern Oregon, offers diverse landscapes and remote backcountry, making it an attractive area for Bigfoot researchers.

Crater Lake National Park

Crater Lake National Park, famous for its stunning lake inside a volcanic crater, has also been mentioned in reports of Bigfoot sightings.

Mount Emily Recreation Area

Mount Emily Recreation Area, located in northeastern Oregon, has been associated with reported Bigfoot encounters.

Ontario, Canada

Ontario's vast and diverse landscapes, which include dense forests, remote wilderness areas, and expansive lakes, have made it an area of interest for reported Bigfoot sightings and encounters.

The Wilderness of Ontario

Ontario's extensive wilderness areas offer plenty of potential habitats for an elusive creature like Bigfoot, attracting researchers and enthusiasts to explore the possibility of its existence.

Algonquin Provincial Park

Algonquin Provincial Park, located in south-central Ontario, is one of the most popular destinations for outdoor enthusiasts. This park has also gained attention for alleged Bigfoot activity and sightings.

Haliburton Forest and Wildlife Reserve

Haliburton Forest and Wildlife Reserve, situated in central Ontario, is known for its vast forested landscapes and diverse wildlife. This region has been associated with reported Bigfoot encounters.

Temagami Wilderness

The Temagami Wilderness, in northeastern Ontario, is another area that has gained attention from Bigfoot researchers.

Georgian Bay Islands National Park

Georgian Bay Islands National Park, located in southeastern Ontario, offers beautiful landscapes and remote areas that have been mentioned in reports of Bigfoot sightings.

Ottawa Valley

The Ottawa Valley, stretching along the Ottawa River, has also been associated with alleged Bigfoot encounters.

Lake Superior Provincial Park

Lake Superior Provincial Park, situated along the northern shores of Lake Superior, is known for its rugged beauty and pristine wilderness. This park has also been mentioned in connection with Bigfoot sightings.

Muskoka Region

The Muskoka region, known for its picturesque lakes and forests, has also gained attention for reported Bigfoot activity.

Killarney Provincial Park

Killarney Provincial Park, in southeastern Ontario, is famous for its stunning landscapes and wilderness. This park has been associated with reported Bigfoot encounters.

Renfrew County

Renfrew County, located in eastern Ontario, has also been mentioned in connection with Bigfoot sightings.

Texas, USA

Texas has attracted attention for claimed Bigfoot sightings and encounters due to its varied environments, which range from thick woods to huge grasslands and rough mountains.

The Lone Star State and Bigfoot

Texas, known as the Lone Star State, has a rich history of folklore and legends, including stories of Bigfoot-like creatures. The state's varied terrain and expansive wilderness provide potential habitats for an elusive creature like Bigfoot.

Big Thicket National Preserve

Big Thicket National Preserve, located in southeastern Texas, is known for its dense forests and diverse wildlife. This region has been associated with reported Bigfoot sightings and encounters.

Sam Houston National Forest

Sam Houston National Forest, situated in east-central Texas, is another area where Bigfoot encounters have been reported. The forest's thick vegetation and remote areas attract researchers and enthusiasts.

Sabine National Forest

Sabine National Forest, located in eastern Texas along the Sabine River, has also been mentioned in reports of Bigfoot-like creatures.

Caddo Lake State Park

Caddo Lake State Park, in northeast Texas, is known for its unique cypress swamp and bayou landscapes. This park has been associated with reported Bigfoot sightings.

Piney Woods Region

The Piney Woods region of eastern Texas, characterized by dense pine forests, has been a location of interest for alleged Bigfoot activity.

Palo Duro Canyon State Park

Palo Duro Canyon State Park, located in the Texas Panhandle, is known for its stunning canyon landscapes. This park has also been mentioned in connection with Bigfoot sightings.

Davis Mountains State Park

Davis Mountains State Park, situated in west Texas, offers rugged mountain terrain and clear night skies. This region has also been associated with reported Bigfoot encounters.

Big Bend National Park

Big Bend National Park, located in southwest Texas, is famous for its dramatic landscapes and remote wilderness. The park has also gained attention for alleged Bigfoot sightings.

South Texas Brush Country

The South Texas Brush Country, characterized by dense vegetation and thorny shrubs, has also been mentioned in connection with Bigfoot encounters.

Respect for Nature and Wildlife

Always respect the environment and wildlife as you explore these Bigfoot hotspots in Texas. Put the preservation of Texas' distinctive landscapes first, adhere to the principles of Leave No Trace, and get the required permits or permissions for research operations.

Florida, USA

While Florida is more commonly associated with its sunny beaches and wetlands, the state's remote and wild areas have also been the site of reported Bigfoot sightings and encounters.

The Sunshine State and Bigfoot

Florida, often referred to as the Sunshine State, is known for its diverse ecosystems, which include marshes, swamps, forests, and prairies. Despite its reputation for sunny beaches and tourist destinations, Florida also has remote wilderness areas that could potentially provide habitats for Bigfoot.

Ocala National Forest

Ocala National Forest, located in north-central Florida, is known for its extensive forested areas and natural springs. This region has been associated with reported Bigfoot sightings and encounters.

Green Swamp Wilderness Preserve

Green Swamp Wilderness Preserve, situated in central Florida, is a large protected area known for its wetlands and diverse wildlife. This region has also been mentioned in connection with Bigfoot sightings.

Myakka River State Park

Myakka River State Park, in southwestern Florida, is known for its expansive wetlands and abundant birdlife. This park has been associated with reported Bigfoot-like creature sightings.

Everglades National Park

Everglades National Park, one of the most iconic wilderness areas in Florida, is famous for its unique ecosystem and diverse wildlife. Although not a traditional Bigfoot hotspot, there have been occasional reports of encounters in this vast wilderness.

Big Cypress National Preserve

Big Cypress National Preserve, located in southern Florida, is known for its cypress swamps and prairies. This preserve has also been mentioned in reports of Bigfoot-like creature sightings.

Apalachicola National Forest

Apalachicola National Forest, in northwestern Florida, is a large expanse of forested land known for its biodiversity. This region has been associated with reported Bigfoot encounters.

St. Johns River Basin

The St. Johns River Basin, stretching across central Florida, has also been mentioned in connection with Bigfoot sightings.

Lake Okeechobee

Lake Okeechobee, the largest freshwater lake in Florida, has been associated with reported Bigfoot-like creature sightings in its surrounding wilderness areas.

Bigfoot in Florida Folklore

Florida's folklore includes stories of "Skunk Ape," a local term for a creature similar to Bigfoot, often associated with sightings in the state's swamps and forests.

New York, USA

New York is a region of interest for claimed Bigfoot sightings and encounters due to its varied landscapes, which include thick woods, mountain ranges, and huge wilderness areas.

The Empire State and Bigfoot

New York, known as the Empire State, is famous for its iconic cities, but it also boasts extensive wilderness areas that could potentially provide habitats for an elusive creature like Bigfoot.

Adirondack Mountains

The Adirondack Mountains, located in upstate New York, are known for their rugged terrain and vast forests. This region has been associated with reported Bigfoot sightings and encounters.

Catskill Mountains

The Catskill Mountains, also in upstate New York, offer a mix of forests and waterways. This area has also been mentioned in connection with Bigfoot sightings.

Allegany State Park

Allegany State Park, situated in southwestern New York, is known for its dense forests and rolling hills. This park has been associated with reported Bigfoot-like creature sightings.

Hudson Valley Region

The Hudson Valley region, stretching along the Hudson River, has been a location of interest for alleged Bigfoot activity.

Taconic Mountains

The Taconic Mountains, located along the eastern border of New York, have also been mentioned in reports of Bigfoot sightings.

Whitehall - Home of the "Whitehall Monster"

The town of Whitehall in upstate New York has gained fame in Bigfoot lore as the home of the "Whitehall Monster," with numerous reported sightings of a creature resembling Bigfoot.

Central New York - The "Southern Tier Sasquatch"

Central New York, including the Southern Tier region, has had reports of Bigfoot-like creatures and is considered a potential hotspot for researchers.

Western New York - The "Chautauqua Lake Monster"

Western New York, including the area around Chautauqua Lake, has also been mentioned in connection with Bigfoot sightings and encounters.

Bigfoot in Native American Folklore

Several Native American tribes in New York, including the Iroquois, have legends and folklore about large, hairy creatures that bear similarities to Bigfoot.

Manitoba, Canada

Bigfoot sightings and interactions have been reported in Manitoba's vast and desolate environment, which encompasses woods, plains, and lakes.

The Wilderness of Manitoba

Manitoba's diverse landscapes offer plenty of potential habitats for an elusive creature like Bigfoot, attracting researchers and enthusiasts to explore its mysteries.
24.2 Riding Mountain National Park
Riding Mountain National Park, located in southwestern Manitoba, is known for its boreal forests and rolling hills. This park has been associated with reported Bigfoot sightings.

Whiteshell Provincial Park

Whiteshell Provincial Park, situated in southeastern Manitoba, is another area where Bigfoot encounters have been reported. The park's diverse landscapes make it an interesting location for researchers.

Duck Mountain Provincial Park

Duck Mountain Provincial Park, in west-central Manitoba, offers a mix of forests, lakes, and hills. This region has also been mentioned in connection with Bigfoot sightings.

Interlake Region

The Interlake region, situated between Lake Manitoba and Lake Winnipeg, has gained attention for alleged Bigfoot activity and sightings.

Mystery Mountain

Mystery Mountain, located in northern Manitoba, is known for its stories of strange occurrences, including reported Bigfoot-like creature sightings.

Lake Manitoba

Lake Manitoba, one of the largest lakes in the province, has also been mentioned in connection with Bigfoot encounters in its surrounding wilderness areas.

Native American and First Nations Legends

Several Native American and First Nations tribes in Manitoba have their own legends and folklore about large, hairy creatures that resemble Bigfoot.

Michigan, USA

Michigan's various landscapes, including dense woods, broad lakeshores, and remote wilderness areas, have made it a popular location for claimed Bigfoot sightings and encounters.

The Great Lakes State and Bigfoot

Michigan, known as the Great Lakes State, is famous for its stunning shoreline along four of the Great Lakes. But beyond its iconic lakeshores, Michigan also offers extensive wilderness areas that could potentially serve as habitats for an elusive creature like Bigfoot.

Upper Peninsula (UP) - The Remote Wilderness

Michigan's Upper Peninsula (UP) is renowned for its remote wilderness, dense forests, and rugged terrain. This region has been associated with numerous reported Bigfoot sightings and encounters.

Huron-Manistee National Forests

The Huron-Manistee National Forests, located in the northern Lower Peninsula and the UP, offer vast forested areas that have been mentioned in connection with Bigfoot activity.

Tahquamenon Falls State Park

Tahquamenon Falls State Park, situated in the UP, is known for its beautiful waterfalls and wilderness. This park has also been associated with reported Bigfoot sightings.

Waterloo-Pinckney Recreation Area

The Waterloo-Pinckney Recreation Area, in southeastern Michigan, is another location that has gained attention from Bigfoot researchers.

Nordhouse Dunes Wilderness Area

The Nordhouse Dunes Wilderness Area, located along the Lake Michigan shoreline, has been mentioned in reports of Bigfoot-like creature sightings.

Allegan State Game Area

Allegan State Game Area, situated in southwestern Michigan, offers dense woodlands and marshes that have been associated with Bigfoot sightings.

Quebec, Canada

Bigfoot sightings and encounters have been reported in Quebec because to the province's large and varied terrain, which include deep woods, isolated wilderness areas, and wide-open waterways.

The Wilderness of Quebec

Quebec's extensive wilderness areas offer plenty of potential habitats for an elusive creature like Bigfoot, attracting researchers and enthusiasts to explore its mysteries.

Mont-Tremblant National Park

Mont-Tremblant National Park, located in the Laurentian Mountains of southern Quebec, is known for its pristine forests and beautiful landscapes. This park has been associated with reported Bigfoot sightings.

Gaspésie National Park

Gaspésie National Park, situated in the Gaspé Peninsula of eastern Quebec, offers rugged terrain and stunning coastal views. This region has also been mentioned in connection with Bigfoot encounters.

Mont Orford National Park

Mont Orford National Park, in the Eastern Townships of southern Quebec, is another area where Bigfoot activity has been reported. Its remote and wooded areas attract outdoor enthusiasts and researchers alike.

Saguenay-Lac-Saint-Jean Region

The Saguenay-Lac-Saint-Jean region, located in the central part of Quebec, has been a location of interest for alleged Bigfoot sightings.

Réserve faunique des Laurentides

The Réserve faunique des Laurentides, situated in the Laurentian Mountains, has also been mentioned in reports of Bigfoot-like creature sightings.

Mauricie National Park

Mauricie National Park, in central Quebec, is known for its vast forests and numerous lakes. This park has been associated with reported Bigfoot encounters.

Abitibi-Témiscamingue Region

The Abitibi-Témiscamingue region, located in western Quebec, has also gained attention for alleged Bigfoot activity.

Northwest Territories, Canada

The Northwest Territories vast and remote wilderness, which includes boreal forests, tundra, and rugged mountains, has made it an area of interest for reported Bigfoot sightings and encounters.

The Wilderness of the Northwest Territories

The Northwest Territories extensive and untamed landscapes offer plenty of potential habitats for an elusive creature like Bigfoot, attracting researchers and enthusiasts to explore its mysteries.

Nahanni National Park Reserve

Nahanni National Park Reserve, located in the southwestern Northwest Territories, is known for its stunning canyons, waterfalls, and boreal forests. This park has been associated with reported Bigfoot-like creature sightings.

Mackenzie Mountains

The Mackenzie Mountains, stretching through the western part of the territory, offer rugged and remote terrain that has been mentioned in connection with Bigfoot encounters.

Great Bear Lake

Great Bear Lake, one of the largest lakes in the world, has also been mentioned in reports of Bigfoot sightings in the surrounding wilderness areas.

Slave Lake Region

The Slave Lake region, situated in the southern part of the territory, has gained attention for alleged Bigfoot activity.

Dehcho Region

The Dehcho region, located in the southwestern part of the territory along the Mackenzie River, has also been a location of interest for Bigfoot researchers.

Tłįchǫ Region

The Tłįchǫ region, inhabited by the Tłįchǫ Dene First Nations, has a rich cultural history with stories of encounters with mysterious creatures, including Bigfoot-like beings.

Gwich'in Region

The Gwich'in region, home to the Gwich'in people, also has cultural stories and folklore related to large, hairy creatures similar to Bigfoot.

Utah, USA

Vast deserts, towering mountains, and dense forests, have made Utah a location of interest for reported Bigfoot sightings and encounters.

The Beehive State and Bigfoot

Utah, known as the Beehive State, is famous for its unique geological formations and outdoor recreational opportunities. While Bigfoot is not typically associated with Utah, there have been occasional reports of sightings and encounters in various parts of the state.

Uinta Mountains

The Uinta Mountains, located in northeastern Utah, are known for their rugged terrain and dense forests. This region has been associated with reported Bigfoot-like creature sightings.

Wasatch Mountains

The Wasatch Mountains, stretching through central Utah, offer beautiful landscapes and abundant wildlife. This area has also been mentioned in connection with Bigfoot sightings.

Manti-La Sal National Forest

Manti-La Sal National Forest, situated in central and southeastern Utah, is known for its diverse ecosystems. This region has also been a location of interest for alleged Bigfoot activity.

High Uintas Wilderness

The High Uintas Wilderness, within the Uinta Mountains, is known for its remote and pristine backcountry. This area has also gained attention from Bigfoot researchers.

Dark Canyon Wilderness

Dark Canyon Wilderness, located in southeastern Utah, offers rugged and isolated terrain. It has been mentioned in reports of Bigfoot encounters.

Indiana, USA

Indiana may not be the first state that comes to mind when thinking about Bigfoot, there have been occasional reports of sightings and encounters in various parts of the state.

The Hoosier State and Bigfoot

Indiana, known as the Hoosier State, is characterized by its rolling farmlands, forests, and waterways. While urban areas dominate much of the state, there are still pockets of wilderness that could potentially provide habitats for an elusive creature like Bigfoot.

Morgan-Monroe State Forest

Morgan-Monroe State Forest, located in south-central Indiana, offers dense woodlands and rugged terrain. This region has been associated with reported Bigfoot sightings.

Hoosier National Forest

Hoosier National Forest, situated in southern Indiana, is another area where Bigfoot encounters have been reported. The forest's diverse landscapes attract outdoor enthusiasts and researchers alike.

Brown County State Park

Brown County State Park, known for its scenic beauty and forested hills, has also been mentioned in connection with Bigfoot sightings.

Yellowwood State Forest

Yellowwood State Forest, located in south-central Indiana, offers a mix of hardwood forests and rolling hills. This region has also been a location of interest for alleged Bigfoot activity.

Native American Legends

Indiana is historically home to Native American tribes, such as the Miami, Potawatomi, and Shawnee. Some of these tribes have legends and folklore about large, hairy creatures that resemble Bigfoot.

Minnesota, USA

Minnesota's diverse landscapes, which include dense forests, numerous lakes, and remote wilderness areas, have made it an intriguing location for reported Bigfoot sightings and encounters.

The Land of 10,000 Lakes and Bigfoot

Minnesota, known as the Land of 10,000 Lakes, is famous for its natural beauty and outdoor recreation opportunities. While Bigfoot may not be the first thing that comes to mind when thinking of Minnesota, there have been occasional reports of sightings and encounters in various parts of the state.

Superior National Forest

Superior National Forest, located in northeastern Minnesota, is known for its vast wilderness and numerous lakes. This region has been associated with reported Bigfoot sightings.

Chippewa National Forest

Chippewa National Forest, situated in north-central Minnesota, offers a mix of forests and wetlands. This area has also been mentioned in connection with Bigfoot encounters.

Itasca State Park

Itasca State Park, in northwestern Minnesota, is famous for being the headwaters of the Mississippi River. This park has been associated with reported Bigfoot-like creature sightings.

Boundary Waters Canoe Area Wilderness (BWCAW)

The Boundary Waters Canoe Area Wilderness, a pristine wilderness area in northeastern Minnesota, has also gained attention from Bigfoot researchers.

Paul Bunyan and Bigfoot Legends

Minnesota's folklore includes stories of Paul Bunyan and Babe the Blue Ox, and some variations of these tales involve encounters with large, hairy creatures similar to Bigfoot.

Native American Legends

Minnesota is home to several Native American tribes, including the Ojibwe and Dakota, who have legends and folklore about large, hairy creatures that resemble Bigfoot.

Nevada, USA

Nevada is a site of interest for claimed Bigfoot sightings and encounters due to its wide and varied landscapes, which include deserts, mountains, and lonely wilderness areas.

The Silver State and Bigfoot

Nevada, known as the Silver State, is famous for its iconic desert landscapes and vibrant city of Las Vegas. While Bigfoot may not be the first thing that comes to mind when thinking of Nevada, there have been occasional reports of sightings and encounters in various parts of the state.

Humboldt-Toiyabe National Forest

Humboldt-Toiyabe National Forest, located in central and eastern Nevada, is known for its rugged terrain and diverse ecosystems. This region has been associated with reported Bigfoot-like creature sightings.

Ruby Mountains

The Ruby Mountains, situated in northeastern Nevada, offer remote and pristine wilderness areas that have been mentioned in connection with Bigfoot encounters.

Area 51 and the Extraterrestrial Highway

Nevada's Area 51, a highly classified military facility, and the nearby Extraterrestrial Highway have gained notoriety for UFO and alien conspiracy theories, but there have also been occasional reports of Bigfoot sightings in this area.

Native American Legends

Nevada is historically home to several Native American tribes, such as the Paiute and Shoshone, who have legends and folklore about large, hairy creatures that resemble Bigfoot.

Montana, USA

Bigfoot sightings and interactions have been reported in Montana because of the state's large and diverse geography, which includes rough mountains, deep forests, and open prairies.

The Treasure State and Bigfoot

Montana, known as the Treasure State, is famous for its natural beauty and abundance of outdoor activities. While Bigfoot may not be the first thing that comes to mind when thinking of Montana, there have been occasional reports of sightings and encounters in various parts of the state.

Bitterroot National Forest

Bitterroot National Forest, located in southwestern Montana, is known for its dense forests and rugged terrain. This region has been associated with reported Bigfoot-like creature sightings.

Gallatin National Forest

Gallatin National Forest, situated in south-central Montana, offers diverse landscapes and abundant wildlife. This area has also been mentioned in connection with Bigfoot sightings.

Flathead National Forest

Flathead National Forest, in northwestern Montana, is another location where Bigfoot encounters have been reported. Its vast wilderness areas attract outdoor enthusiasts and researchers alike.

Glacier National Park

Glacier National Park, located in northwestern Montana, is famous for its stunning glaciers and pristine wilderness. This park has also been associated with reported Bigfoot sightings.

Native American Legends

Montana is home to several Native American tribes, such as the Blackfeet and Crow, who have legends and folklore about large, hairy creatures that resemble Bigfoot.

Oklahoma, USA

Welcome to Chapter 24 of "The Bigfoot Hunters Handbook." In this chapter, we will explore some of the well-known Bigfoot hotspots in Oklahoma. While Oklahoma may not be as widely associated with Bigfoot as some other states, there have been occasional reports of sightings and encounters in various parts of the state.

The Sooner State and Bigfoot

Oklahoma, known as the Sooner State, is characterized by its diverse landscapes, including forests, plains, and rolling hills. While urban areas dominate much of the state, there are still areas of wilderness that could potentially provide habitats for an elusive creature like Bigfoot.

Ouachita National Forest

Ouachita National Forest, located in southeastern Oklahoma, is known for its rugged mountains and dense woodlands. This region has been associated with reported Bigfoot sightings.

Wichita Mountains Wildlife Refuge

Wichita Mountains Wildlife Refuge, in southwestern Oklahoma, offers a mix of prairies and forested hills. This area has also been mentioned in connection with Bigfoot encounters.

Cherokee Nation and Native American Legends

Oklahoma is home to numerous Native American tribes, including the Cherokee Nation, who have their own legends and folklore about large, hairy creatures that resemble Bigfoot.

Georgia, USA

Georgia's, mountains, forests, and swamps, have made it a location of interest for reported Bigfoot sightings and encounters.

The Peach State and Bigfoot

Georgia, known as the Peach State, is famous for its southern charm and historical significance. While Bigfoot may not be the first thing that comes to mind when thinking of Georgia, there have been occasional reports of sightings and encounters in various parts of the state.

Chattahoochee National Forest

Chattahoochee National Forest, located in northern Georgia, is known for its vast woodlands and rugged terrain. This region has been associated with reported Bigfoot-like creature sightings.

Okefenokee Swamp

The Okefenokee Swamp, situated in southeastern Georgia, offers dense wilderness and waterways. This area has also been mentioned in connection with Bigfoot sightings.

Blue Ridge Mountains

The Blue Ridge Mountains, stretching through northern Georgia, are another location where Bigfoot encounters have been reported. The mountains' remote areas attract outdoor enthusiasts and researchers alike.

Native American Legends

Georgia is historically home to several Native American tribes, such as the Cherokee and Cree, who have legends and folklore about large, hairy creatures that resemble Bigfoot.

Illinois, USA

Illinois is not typically associated with Bigfoot as much as some other states, but there have been occasional reports of sightings and encounters in various parts of the state.

The Prairie State and Bigfoot

Illinois, known as the Prairie State, is characterized by its fertile plains, forests, and urban areas. While the state's landscape is more associated with agricultural activities, there have been reports of Bigfoot-like creatures in certain areas.

Shawnee National Forest

Shawnee National Forest, located in southern Illinois, offers dense woodlands and rugged terrain. This region has been associated with reported Bigfoot sightings.

Cache River State Natural Area

The Cache River State Natural Area, in southern Illinois, is known for its unique wetlands and wildlife. This area has also been mentioned in connection with Bigfoot encounters.

Native American Legends

Illinois is historically home to Native American tribes, including the Illinois Confederation and the Kickapoo, who have legends and folklore about large, hairy creatures that resemble Bigfoot.

Wisconsin, USA

Wisconsin's forests, lakes, and rural areas, have made it an intriguing location for reported Bigfoot sightings and encounters.

The Badger State and Bigfoot

Wisconsin, known as the Badger State, is famous for its dairy farms, rolling hills, and natural beauty. While Bigfoot may not be the first thing that comes to mind when thinking of Wisconsin, there have been occasional reports of sightings and encounters in various parts of the state.

Chequamegon-Nicolet National Forest

Chequamegon-Nicolet National Forest, located in northern Wisconsin, is known for its extensive woodlands and diverse wildlife. This region has been associated with reported Bigfoot-like creature sightings.

Kettle Moraine State Forest

Kettle Moraine State Forest, situated in southeastern Wisconsin, offers beautiful glacial landforms and wooded areas. This area has also been mentioned in connection with Bigfoot sightings.

Native American Legends

Wisconsin is historically home to several Native American tribes, such as the Ojibwe and Menominee, who have legends and folklore about large, hairy creatures that resemble Bigfoot.

Door County Peninsula

The Door County Peninsula, a popular tourist destination in eastern Wisconsin, has also gained attention from Bigfoot researchers.

Pennsylvania, USA

If you're interested in exploring potential Bigfoot hotspots in Pennsylvania, here are a few areas where sightings and reports have been more common:

Allegheny National Forest:

This vast forested region in northwestern Pennsylvania has been the site of numerous Bigfoot sightings over the years. The remote and heavily wooded areas provide suitable habitat for such a creature.

Michaux State Forest:

Located in south-central Pennsylvania, Michaux State Forest has also been the site of reported Bigfoot encounters. The rugged terrain and dense woods make it a possible habitat for cryptids.

Chestnut Ridge:

This ridge runs through several counties in southwestern Pennsylvania, and it has a history of Bigfoot sightings and other paranormal activity. It's sometimes referred to as the "UFO capital of Pennsylvania," but Bigfoot reports are not uncommon here.

Delaware Water Gap National Recreation Area:

This area along the Pennsylvania-New Jersey border features a mix of dense forests and rugged terrain, which some believe could provide a suitable habitat for Bigfoot.

Fayette County:

There have been reports of Bigfoot sightings in various parts of Fayette County, located in southwestern Pennsylvania.

Susquehannock State Forest:

This forested region in north-central Pennsylvania has also been the location of reported Bigfoot sightings.